Humanitarian Intervention and Political Support for Interstate Use of Force

Nijhoff Law Specials

VOLUME 101

The titles published in this series are listed at *brill.com/nlsp*

Humanitarian Intervention and Political Support for Interstate Use of Force

Edited by

Cyrille Fijnaut
Joris Larik

BRILL
NIJHOFF

LEIDEN | BOSTON

Library of Congress Control Number: 2020949208

Typeface for the Latin, Greek, and Cyrillic scripts: "Brill". See and download: brill.com/brill-typeface.

ISSN 0924-4549
ISBN 978-90-04-44547-5 (paperback)
ISBN 978-90-04-44548-2 (e-book)

This book is printed on acid-free paper and produced in a sustainable manner.

Expert Group on Political Support for Interstate Use of Force and on Humanitarian Intervention

Chair

Prof. Dr. Cyrille Fijnaut

Members of the Expert Group

Mr. Kristian Fischer

Prof. Dr. Terry Gill

Prof. Dr. Larissa van den Herik

Prof. Dr. Martti Koskenniemi

Prof. Dr. Claus Kreß

Mr. Robert Serry

Ms. Monika Sie Dhian Ho

Ms. Elizabeth Wilmshurst

Prof. Dr. Rob de Wijk

Secretariat

Dr. Joris Larik

Ms. Nienke van Heukelingen

Table of Contents

Foreword

It is an atrocity etched in our collective memory: the horrific poison gas attack in Douma, Syria, in 2018, which caused immense human suffering. The attack was a grave violation of the prohibition on the use of chemical weapons. The Dutch government regarded the military intervention by the United States, the United Kingdom and France in response to the attack as both well considered and proportionate. However, since there was no basis in international law for the intervention, the government was unable to give its political support. Since the publication of the Davids Committee report in 2010, such political support must always have a basis in international law.

Unfortunately, we live in an era in which countries use their UN Security Council veto to hamper investigations into those responsible for violations and to block unified action aimed at reducing humanitarian suffering. Given the current geopolitical context, it is conceivable that the Netherlands could again be confronted with a situation in which we are asked to lend political support for the use of force between states in the absence of a basis in international law.

When can the Netherlands give political support to a military intervention in another state? The answer to this question is extremely complex, topical and time-sensitive. For these reasons, I commissioned an Expert Group on Political Support for the Use of Force Between States and Humanitarian Intervention to reexamine this matter. In addition, I asked the group to consider whether the Netherlands should press for international acceptance of humanitarian intervention as a possible new legal basis for the use of force between states in exceptional circumstances.

The Expert Group's thorough analysis and recommendations on this complex subject offer important insights that can aid the government in formulating its position on political support for the use of force between states and humanitarian intervention. In drawing up this advisory report the Expert Group has helped the government develop a new, contemporary vision on these issues, a vision it describes in its response to the report, which was sent to the House of Representatives on 17 April 2020. I would like to sincerely thank the members of the Expert Group, which was led by Professor Cyrille Fijnaut, for their valuable contribution.

This advisory report can also be a useful tool for others in considering these difficult issues and as such enable us to continue working together to ensure a world in which international law is respected by all.

Stef Blok
Minister of Foreign Affairs of the Kingdom of the Netherlands

Preface

The Minister of Foreign Affairs of the Netherlands, Stef Blok, by his Order of 25 April 2019, established an Expert Group on Political Support for Interstate Use of Force and on Humanitarian Intervention. The Expert Group was tasked with giving its opinion(s) on (a) the government's expression of political support for the use of force between states without a basis in international law; and (b) whether the Dutch government should promote the international acceptance of humanitarian intervention as a possible new legal basis for the interstate use of force.

In the explanatory notes to the Order, the government states that the Expert Group is to produce an advisory report in an expeditious manner without, however, sacrificing quality and depth. The Expert Group started its work on 1 June 2019 and concluded its deliberations on 19 November 2019. Its composition is included in Annex A.

The fact that the Expert Group was able to meet the government's timetable was not only the result of its working methods, which will be explained in the introduction of the report, but also of a number of other factors that we would like to highlight.

First of all, it has to be emphasized that the logistical preparations carried out by the Ministry of Foreign Affairs, in particular by Erik van Uum and Kevin Brongers, and subsequently by Sladjana Cemerikic and Wibe van der Linden, greatly facilitated the work of the Expert Group and its secretariat.

Secondly, we want to express our gratitude to Prof. Dr. Erwin Muller, Dean of the Faculty of Governance and Global Affairs, and to Henriët Reininga from Leiden University's Buildings & Facilities Service. Their willingness to house the secretariat of the Expert Group at the premises of Leiden University's Campus The Hague made the organization of our internal meetings and research activities considerably easier.

Thirdly, we would like to acknowledge the efforts of Steve Lambley, copyeditor, and Raymond Swart, graphic designer, who made it possible to produce this report in a short period of time.

The Hague, 19 November 2019

Prof. Dr. Cyrille Fijnaut, chair

Dr. Joris Larik, secretary

Executive Summary

By Order of 25 April 2019, the Minister of Foreign Affairs, Stef Blok, established the present Expert Group, requesting it to offer its views on the following two questions: on the one hand, lending of political support by the Dutch government to the interstate use of force by other states without a basis in international law; on the other, whether the Netherlands should strive for international acceptance of humanitarian intervention as a possible new legal basis for the use of force between states in exceptional circumstances.

Following the chair's work plan, which included background research by the secretariat, position papers by the members and a meeting in The Hague on 6–8 October 2019, the Expert Group finalized its report in an expedient manner.

The report recalls the background of the current Dutch position on the matters raised in the questions addressed to the Expert Group and the international context into which the issues at stake have to be situated (see chapter 2). This includes the international legal framework, geopolitical developments, ongoing reform efforts and proposals and the difficulty of defining success when it comes to interstate use of force and humanitarian intervention.

In answer to the question regarding whether the Dutch government should promote the international acceptance of humanitarian intervention as a possible new legal basis for interstate use of force (see chapter 3), the Expert Group considers that existing international law concerning the use of force by states contains only two firmly accepted exceptions to the general prohibition to use force under Article 2, paragraph 4 of the Charter of the United Nations. These are the use of force under the authority of the United Nations Security Council (Articles 39–42 of the UN Charter) and use of force in self-defence (Article 51 of the UN Charter). However, a minority is of the view that in light of the practice of states, it is no longer possible to conclude that forcible action to defend a civilian population in case of a most serious attack is manifestly unlawful if undertaken as a last resort and under strict conditions.

As far as the question as to whether the Dutch government should seek another exception with the view of allowing the use of force by states for ostensibly humanitarian purposes is concerned, the great majority is of the view that it did not seem advisable at present. It does not seem possible or desirable to seek such an exception for both legal and political reasons. Instead, the Expert Group advises that it might be useful if the Dutch government were to take steps to initiate informal consultations, within the context of the European Union and NATO, and with other like-minded and interested countries on ways to deal with humanitarian emergencies. The Expert Group emphasizes the importance of inclusive discussions on this matter at a global level as well.

A minority is of the view that such informal consultations could include an effort to explore whether and how conditions could be formulated under which forcible action in defence of a civilian population under a most serious attack, if undertaken under strict conditions, might not be unlawful even in the absence of authorization by the United Nations Security Council. Those conditions might include the likelihood that forcible action will be successful in avoiding or at least strictly limiting civilian casualties.

In answer to the question regarding the government's expression of political support for the use of force between states without a basis in international law (see chapter 4), the Expert Group stresses that there is a clear distinction between, on the one hand, offering support, such as troops, arms or logistics, which would trigger state responsibility for the commission of unlawful acts, and, on the other, offering political support in a political forum, which would not. In addition, mere political support by government officials after the commission of an unlawful act by another government does not lead to those officials incurring individual criminal responsibility under the Rome Statute of the International Criminal Court.

Nevertheless, even though a state offering political support does not incur responsibility under international law, the Expert Group is of the view that there are strong legal and political reasons for exercising caution before supporting a military operation which the Netherlands regards as unlawful. Ignoring the applicability of the law by supporting unlawful actions risks the erosion of the international legal order and may encourage future unlawful behaviour.

Having taken the legal and political risks and consequences into account, the government may nonetheless find that there are compelling reasons to offer political support to an intervention even though they regard it as unlawful. The kind of circumstances that may be regarded as meriting such support may relate to extreme humanitarian distress, including the use of chemical weapons with direct danger for civilians.

1. Introduction

1. On 25 April 2019, the Minister of Foreign Affairs, Stef Blok, established the present Expert Group, which was requested to offer its views on the following two questions:
   - the lending of political support by the Dutch government to the interstate use of force by other states without a basis in international law;
   - whether the Netherlands should strive for international acceptance of humanitarian intervention as a possible new legal basis for the use of force between states in exceptional circumstances.

2. In an earlier letter of 10 December 2018 to the Dutch House of Representatives explaining the background for establishing the Expert Group, the Minister referred to the Dutch position in relation to the response of the United States, the United Kingdom and France to the poison gas attack on Douma, Syria. The Netherlands expressed its "understanding" (*begrip*) for this response and judged it to be "proportional and well-considered", as the Netherlands believes that it is vital that the international community vigorously upholds the norm of international law that chemical weapons must never be used. The Minister explained in the letter that the Dutch government had difficulties with the statement as adopted by the North Atlantic Council (NAC) expressing "full support" (*volledige steun*) for the actions of the named countries. In the explanation of its vote within the NAC, the Netherlands stated that, despite its concerns, it voted in favour of the NAC's statement on the grounds of North Atlantic Treaty Organization (NATO) solidarity. The Netherlands was the only NATO member state to issue such an explanation of its vote.

3. The Dutch position on this matter was informed by the lessons learnt from the Dutch Iraq Inquiry under the chairmanship of Willibrord Davids (the Davids Committee). The Davids Committee held in 2010 that there had not been an adequate legal basis for the invasion of Iraq. In response to the findings of the Davids Committee, the Dutch government explicitly confirmed that the requirement of an adequate legal basis also applies to situations in which the Netherlands offers political support to other states undertaking military action. It seems that the government now wishes to revisit this confirmation, leading to the first question on which advice has been sought.

4. The second question asks whether the Netherlands should make efforts towards the acceptance of humanitarian intervention as a new legal basis

 DOI:10.1163/9789004445482_002

for the use of force between states. Seeing that this question is of a more systemic nature and that the answer to it also informs the answer to the first question, the Expert Group decided to reverse the original order of questions.

5. Article 7 of the Order by which the Expert Group was established states that the chair is to determine the working methods of the Expert Group and will provide an account thereof in the final report. In the explanatory notes of the Order, it is added that the chair is to gather the views and opinions of the members of the Expert Group and synthetize them in a report. This is also why, unlike other advisory committees, the Expert Group would only meet once. Moreover, according to the explanatory notes, the opinions and insights gathered by the chair are first to be presented to the members for comment, before being incorporated into the final report.

6. In conformity with these provisions, the chair outlined the following working methods to the members of the Expert Group in his letter of 7 June 2019:

   - the members were asked to identify by 15 July 2019 the most relevant pieces of literature in order to build a common body of knowledge for reference; these pieces would be included in a reader that in its turn would be sent to the members by the end of July;
   - in parallel with the composition of the syllabus, the chair and the secretary would prepare a bibliography that covers the most relevant books, reports, articles and contributions that have been published in recent years;
   - in order to further the preparatory work of the members, the chair and secretary would write and share background notes, respectively on the background and context of the Dutch position concerning the 14 April 2018 military response to the attack on Douma, Syria, of 7 April 2018, in which chemical weapons were used, and on the legal framework and the contemporary academic debate regarding interstate use of force and humanitarian intervention;
   - with a view to the collection of the views and opinions of the members of the Expert Group, members were asked to prepare a position paper on the issues at stake before 31 August 2019;
   - these views and opinions would be synthetized in mid-September 2019 in a working document and collated in a syllabus, both of which would be transmitted to the members of the Expert Group;

- the Expert Group would meet on 6–8 October in The Hague to discuss, on the basis of the position papers, the working document as well as the background notes, the answers to the questions the government had addressed to it.

By virtue of a total of five successive updates, the chair ensured that the proposed way of working was implemented in an expedient and timely manner.

7. The discussion of the Expert Group in The Hague resulted in the final report in two stages. At the meeting in The Hague, the Expert Group could come to an agreement on the answers to the two questions. These are included in chapters 3 and 4 of this report. At the same time, it could agree upon a division of tasks among the members in relation to the text of chapter 2. The proposals made by the members for the text of this chapter were integrated by the chair into the draft of this chapter. The draft report was sent to the members on 29 October 2019. After their comments were integrated, the final report was transmitted to the copyeditor on 19 November 2019.

8. In relation to the way in which the Expert Group has executed its mandate, it is important to recall that according to Article 3, paragraph 2 of the Order establishing the Expert Group, the chair, the members and the secretariat participate in their personal capacity and discharge their duties independently and without instructions or consultation. Moreover, the Minister of Foreign Affairs wrote in his letter of 23 May 2019 to the members that “the report does not have to be univocal or conclusive”. These basic parameters of the Expert Group’s work ensured that its deliberations took place in an open-minded and constructive environment. This, in turn, allowed the completion of the report within a limited timeframe in a way that draws on the members’ multinational and multidisciplinary backgrounds as well as their different professional experiences.

9. The structure of the report is as follows. Following this introduction, chapter 2 outlines in broad terms the Dutch position and the international context into which the issues at stake have to be situated. Chapter 3 contains the answer to the question with regard to the promotion of humanitarian intervention as a possible new exception to the general prohibition to use force in international law. Chapter 4 provides the answer to the question of political support for interstate use of force without a basis in international law. Annexed to the report are the following documents: the composition of the Expert Group (A.), a timeline of events (B.), extracts from the UN Charter and other relevant documents (C.), notes on the background

and context of the Dutch position (D.) and on the legal framework and academic discourse (E.), and the bibliography (F.).

2. The Dutch Position in its International Context

10. The Dutch position on the matters of political support for interstate use of force and humanitarian intervention needs to be seen in its international context, both legal and political. Hence, before turning to its findings, the report first outlines the international legal framework relating to the use of armed force, the geopolitical context, relevant ongoing reform efforts and proposals, and addresses the difficulty of defining success in cases of interstate use of force and humanitarian intervention.

International Legal Framework

11. The cornerstone of the current international legal order is the prohibition of the threat or use of force contained in Article 2, paragraph 4 of the UN Charter. This provision lays down a comprehensive ban on the threat or use of armed force between states or across an international border for any purpose other than the exceptions contained in the UN Charter itself. In brief, it bans the use of armed force except when authorized by the UN Security Council or when necessary in self-defence. States may use force in self-defence, both individually (by one state in response to an armed attack originating from outside its borders) and collectively (by more than one state in response to an armed attack against one or more of them). The use of force in self-defence falls outside the purview of this advice and will receive no further attention here.

12. In addition to the two firmly accepted exceptions of (1) Security Council authorization and (2) self-defence provided for in the UN Charter, it has been argued by some that the use of force as a measure of last resort to halt large scale atrocities in situations where neither (1) nor (2) is applicable has become lawful or can no longer be considered to be unambiguously unlawful due to the subsequent practice of states. It has also been suggested by some that it would be desirable as a matter of legal policy if the use of force in such a case became lawful in the future. No agreement on these suggestions has been reached, but the discussion is ongoing, as can be seen, for instance, from the 2018 report of the International Law Association's Committee on the Use of Force. In 2005, the heads of state and government gathered at the United Nations Headquarters for the World Summit endorsed provisions of the UN Charter for the use of force and did not recognize any exception to the prohibition of the use of force other than (1) and (2) above.

 | DOI:10.1163/9789004445482_003

13. A breach by a state of the prohibition of the threat or use of force in Article 2, paragraph 4 of the UN Charter entails the international responsibility of that state. Such responsibility may lead to the state being held liable for reparations to the injured state.

14. A serious breach of the prohibition of the use of force under Article 2, paragraph 4 of the UN Charter may amount to aggression. Aggression involves a breach of a so-called peremptory norm of international law (*ius cogens*). Article 53 of the Vienna Convention of the Law of Treaties defines a peremptory norm as "accepted and recognized by the international community of states as a whole as a norm from which no derogation is permitted and which can be modified only by a subsequent norm of general international law having the same character". Treaties that conflict with *ius cogens* norms are void (Articles 53 and 64 of the Vienna Convention of the Law of Treaties). Breach of a peremptory norm triggers the duty of all states to bring the breach to an end. It is contrary at least to the spirit of that duty to voice political support for such a breach.

15. State officials in leadership, who take part in the planning, preparation, initiation or execution of a serious breach of the prohibition of the use of force by their state, can be criminally liable for a crime of aggression under international criminal law as defined in Article 8*bis* of the Rome Statute of the International Criminal Court. Under certain circumstances, these officials may be prosecuted by the International Criminal Court.

Geopolitical Context

16. Due to geopolitical shifts, reaching consensus on UN Security Council Resolutions will likely be more difficult. Since 2010, the United States has exercised its veto power three times, the Russian Federation eighteen times, of which eight times were together with China. France and the United Kingdom have not used their veto in the Security Council since 1989.

17. China is rising to superpower status and will make its mark on the international order. Like the United Kingdom and the United States after the end of the Second World War, Beijing seeks to adapt the present rules-based order in such a way that it reflects its interests, positions and values. In doing so, China questions Western values and prevailing interpretations of international law. For example, China sees human rights more in terms of collective rights such as security, stability and prosperity. China supports a rather strict interpretation of sovereignty.

18. China is willing to support UN Security Council mandates for traditional peacekeeping operations. Those mandates should reflect three inter-related and mutually reinforcing principles: consent of the parties; impartiality of the peacekeepers; and the non-use of force except in cases of self-defence and defence of the mandate. China is likely to reject unmandated interventions for humanitarian purposes. Only in very rare circumstances could China be willing to support Western military action other than peacekeeping. The best the Western members of the Security Council can usually hope for are abstentions.

19. As a result of the changing geopolitical environment, Russia and possibly other powers will be less constrained in their foreign policies. As Russia's official position on non-interference is quite similar to that of China, the Kremlin is likely to block Western proposals for mandated interventions as well, as evidenced most notably by the use of its veto powers in the context of the conflict in Syria.

20. Anti-Western sentiments and mistrust, which are rooted in perceived double standards, colonialism, imperialism and interventionism, are an obstacle for obtaining mandates as well. The intervention in Libya is a case in point. In 2010 and 2011, NATO member states decided to stop the Libyan leader Colonel Gaddafi terrorizing his people. The resulting intervention was supported by UN Security Council Resolution 1973 (2011), but Russia and China, among others, protested that the use of force amounted to regime change in excess of the mandate. When those states blocked subsequent mandates for intervention, they also referred to the Libyan experience. The Libya case thus added to the mistrust caused by the first "humanitarian war", i.e. the 1999 NATO Kosovo war that took place without UN Security Council authorization.

21. The different strategic outlooks of China and Russia notwithstanding, their approaches regarding UN Security Council resolutions complicate the calculus and freedom to manoeuvre of Western powers. In the case of Russia, this includes an increased willingness to take military action in support of a friendly regime or insurgency movement. For example, in 2015 President Bashar al-Assad as the head of the government of Syria invited Russia to intervene in his country and justified its military involvement there. At the same time, both Syria and Russia argued that the use of force by the US-led coalition was illegal. Thus, the changed balance of forces and the legal arguments confronted the anti-Assad coalition with important political, ethical and military dilemmas. Due to the global power shifts, this is likely to happen more often in the future.

Reform Efforts and Initiatives at UN Level

22. The Expert Group recalls that the questions about political support for interstate use of force and humanitarian intervention also need to be seen in the light of ongoing discussions and reform initiatives in multilateral frameworks. Rather than the unavailability of a legal basis in international law, the failure to prevent and inaction of the Security Council in the face of mass atrocities should be seen as the primary sources of concern.

23. Efforts in this domain include the implementation of the Responsibility to Protect (R2P) principles, making better use of inter-institutional dynamics at the United Nations and proposals for strengthening the transparency and effectiveness of the Security Council in its responses to mass atrocities. The Expert Group submits that these different initiatives, and their interaction, have the potential to contribute to preventing and effectively responding to international crises and mass atrocities within the existing framework of international law.

24. The Expert Group recalls that the 2005 World Summit Outcome document officially affirmed the principles of R2P as a duty to use diplomatic, humanitarian and other peaceful means to help to protect populations from genocide, war crimes, ethnic cleansing and crimes against humanity. This can entail collective action, through the Security Council and in accordance with Chapter VII of the United Nations Charter, where peaceful means are inadequate and national authorities are manifestly failing to protect their populations. The R2P principles have been referred to on numerous occasions by the Security Council, the General Assembly and the Human Rights Council ever since. The UN Secretary-General, in subsequent reports on R2P, has stressed the particular importance of prevention in this context. The more effective prevention and early warning mechanisms become, the less need there will be for interstate use of force to address humanitarian crises.

25. The question was raised in the Expert Group as to what extent the subsidiary responsibilities of the UN General Assembly and the Secretary-General in the area of international peace and security, as laid down in the UN Charter, could be used more proactively to overcome Security Council inaction. For example, certain steps and procedures in accordance with the UN Charter could be envisaged for the General Assembly to consider a report by the Secretary-General on a given humanitarian crisis situation, which in his/her view poses a threat to international peace and security. With a two-thirds majority, the General Assembly can adopt a resolution requesting the Security Council to consider the report and take appropriate action.

26. In addition, with a view to improving the effectiveness and transparency of the way the Security Council operates, different proposals have been put forward by states. These include the Accountability, Coherence and Transparency (ACT) group, which calls for the adoption of a voluntary code of conduct to restrain the use of veto powers, and the French-Mexican political declaration asking the permanent members of the Security Council to pledge to refrain from using the veto in case of recognized mass atrocities.

The Definition of Success

27. A reasonable expectation of success should be taken into account when supporting military action politically. In practice, this key requirement is often underestimated. Although a decision "to do something" could be morally right initially, failure could result in grave political consequences.

28. Success can be measured in relation to the declared objectives of the intervener such as the relief of humanitarian suffering or preventing the use of unlawful weapons. Declared political objectives are a prerequisite for defining the military means needed. Indeed, the old Clausewitzian dictum of the need to balance military means against political objectives explains why interventions and military operations are successes or failures. Moreover, it should be taken into account in this context that decisions regarding military intervention involve difficult dilemmas and often need to be taken within a limited timeframe to consider these dilemmas and, therefore, on the basis of limited information.

29. On the one hand, interventions such as those in Sierra Leone (2000) and Côte d'Ivoire (2002) were to a large degree successful. On the other hand, the interventions in Afghanistan (2001), Iraq (2003) and Libya (2011) resulted in regime changes but the subsequent stabilization operations dragged on for years or were not carried out at all (Libya). The narrow political objective of regime change required a limited number of forces for a short period of time, but the subsequent stabilization mission required very large numbers of forces that could not be sustained for a prolonged period of time.

30. Moreover, balancing means and ends is particularly difficult in complex contingencies, which "combine internal conflicts with large-scale displacements of people, mass famine, and fragile or failing economic, political, and social institutions", as noted already in the 1995 report *Global Humanitarian Emergencies* published by the US Mission to the UN. Such situations could emerge after a regime change. But also years of conflict and persecution, often fuelled by the motives of political entrepreneurs, could cause a breakdown of government and chronic insecurity. Eruptions

of violence could also follow from the deliberate responses of determined leaders concerning corruption, discrimination, economic failure, maladministration, repression and poor economic conditions.

31. Complex contingencies very rarely involve regular armies on both sides. As can be seen from the annual yearbooks published by the Stockholm International Peace Research Institute (SIPRI), in those circumstances, low-intensity war will replace high-intensity interstate warfare almost completely because opponents are likely to fight only asymmetrical wars. Due to Western superiority in combat power, adversaries have no other choice but to use the "great equalizer" to thwart the West's superiority: unconventional and asymmetrical strategies of counter-coercion, as a result of which the distinction between combatants and non-combatants becomes blurred. If this is done in a smart way, the West's military might scarcely matters. Consequently, the intervention may fail.

32. In sum, "doing something" or engaging in a military operation might lead to a number of severe consequences. "Doing something" could be morally right initially but supporting such a course of action involves considerable political risks. An intervention may fail because it is justified on moral grounds and decision-makers focus too much on the justification and the legal aspects of interventions and ignore international repercussions, the conflict dynamics, the balance between political ends and military means and the efficacy of the military action.

3. Findings on the Question of Humanitarian Intervention

33. This section sets out the findings of the Expert Group regarding the question as to whether the Netherlands should strive for international acceptance of humanitarian intervention as a possible new legal basis for the use of force between states in exceptional circumstances.

34. The Expert Group considers that existing international law concerning the use of force by states contains only two firmly accepted exceptions to the general prohibition to use force under Article 2, paragraph 4 of the UN Charter. These are the use of force under the authority of the United Nations Security Council (Articles 39–42) and use of force in self-defence (Article 51). However, a minority is of the view that in light of the practice of states it is no longer possible to conclude that forcible action to defend a civilian population in case of a most serious attack is manifestly unlawful if undertaken as a last resort and under strict conditions.

35. The great majority is of the view that it does not seem advisable at present for the Dutch government to seek another exception with the view of allowing the use of force by states for ostensibly humanitarian purposes. It does not seem possible or desirable to seek such exception for the following reasons:

   - the general prohibition to use force in international relations is a norm of fundamental importance for the international community;
   - it would not be likely to receive the broad support of the international community in the foreseeable future;
   - experience shows that military interventions can also create negative consequences that cannot be foreseen as they are planned; and
   - even limited exceptions are likely to be used for purposes not originally envisaged by those who adopt them.

36. In view of the above conclusions, it might be useful if the Dutch government were to take steps to initiate informal consultations, within the context of the European Union (EU) and NATO, and with other like-minded and interested countries on ways to deal with humanitarian emergencies. The Expert Group emphasizes the importance of having inclusive discussions on this matter at a global level as well.

37. A minority is of the view that such informal consultations could include an effort to explore whether and how conditions could be formulated under

 | DOI:10.1163/9789004445482_004

which forcible action in defence of a civilian population under the most serious attack, if undertaken under strict conditions, might not be unlawful even in the absence of a United Nations Security Council authorization. Those conditions might include the likelihood that forcible action will be successful in avoiding or at least strictly limiting civilian casualties.

38. The Dutch government could also pursue all avenues for developing existing mechanisms for dealing with humanitarian emergencies such as strengthening the decision-making capacities of the Security Council, including on the basis of existing initiatives for codes of conduct on Security Council voting in the face of mass atrocities.

39. The government is also recommended to engage with members of the United Nations Security Council and other members of the United Nations to encourage the use of Responsibility to Protect (R2P) principles.

40. The Dutch government could also examine possibilities under the UN Charter for developing existing mechanisms for dealing with humanitarian emergencies such as procedures and steps to be taken under the auspices of the UN General Assembly, the good offices of the Secretary-General, regional organizations and arrangements under Chapter VIII of the UN Charter.

4. Findings on the Question of Political Support

41. This section presents the Expert Group's findings regarding the question as to whether the Dutch government should lend political support for the interstate use of force by other states for which there is no basis in international law. This question does not cover the issue of non-lethal assistance to non-state armed opposition groups. Nor does it concern direct participation in military operations or questions of self-defence.

42. Within the Expert Group the question was raised as to whether a state lending political support for the use of force without a legal basis could incur responsibility under international law. In particular, the Articles on State Responsibility for Internationally Wrongful Acts – Article 16 on aid or assistance, or complicity, and Article 41, paragraph 2 containing the obligation not to recognize unlawful situations – might be relevant.

43. The Expert Group is of the clear view that merely providing political support subsequent to an unlawful action does not incur international legal responsibility for the supporting state. Article 16 concerns actual aid or assistance, as it requires that the support facilitated the commission of the wrongful act and significantly contributed to it. Article 41, paragraph 2, in turn, addresses a situation different from the offering of political support to an illegal act. As is clearly indicated by its wording, it is an obligation not to recognize the *unlawful situation arising from* the breach. It thus concerns the consequences of the breach rather than the breach itself.

44. There is consequently a clear distinction between, on the one hand, offering support, such as troops, arms or logistics, which would trigger state responsibility for the commission of unlawful acts, and, on the other, offering political support in a political forum, which would not. In addition, mere political support by government officials after the commission of an unlawful act by another government does not lead to those officials incurring individual criminal responsibility under the Rome Statute of the International Criminal Court.

45. Nevertheless, even though a state offering political support does not incur responsibility under international law, there are strong reasons for exercising caution before supporting a military operation which the Netherlands regards as unlawful.

46. In the first place, there are legal risks in offering support for interventions without a basis in international law:

 | DOI:10.1163/9789004445482_005

- Following the Second World War, the universal acceptance by the international community of the prohibition on the use of force represented a huge gain for an international rules-based society. Ignoring the applicability of the law by supporting unlawful actions risks the erosion of the international legal order.

- Political support for another state's use of force, combined with a lack of expression of disagreement with its postulated legal basis, may be taken by the international community as meaning that the supporting government agrees with the legal basis for the action. This may make it more difficult in the future for that government to express disagreement with another state's actions.

- Such support may also encourage future unlawful behaviour and contribute to a culture in which states intending to use force in similar circumstances in the future will believe themselves unlikely to meet a negative international response.

- The credibility of governments that normally assert the importance of international law would be strained if they regularly failed to respond in any way to the commission of illegal acts.

47. Secondly, there may be political consequences: the government must accept responsibility for repercussions that their political support will have on international relations in the broad sense and on concrete relationships in particular.

48. Having taken these legal and political risks and consequences into account, the government may nonetheless find that there are compelling reasons to offer political support to an intervention, even though they regard it as unlawful. The kind of circumstances that may be regarded as meriting such support may relate to extreme humanitarian distress, including the use of chemical weapons with direct danger for civilians.

49. Relevant considerations in deciding to offer political support in such extreme circumstances might include the relationship with allies, and the necessary and proportionate scope of the intervention, together with the absence of any alternative course of action, including as a result of the use of the veto in the Security Council. Also relevant are the need for clear objectives, a reasonable prospect of success for the intervention itself and the reasonably foreseeable consequences of that intervention.

50. In the light of the above, the caution exercised by the government in deciding whether to offer political support should not only relate to the making of a supportive statement but should also inform the choice of wording. It is recognized that decisions may have to be taken under pressure and

with strong time constraints. Decisions will have to be taken on a case by case basis.

51. The government is not alone in wishing on occasion to offer political support for another country's military operation while at the same time doubting the legal basis for it. It is recommended that the government enter into consultations with allies within NATO and the EU in order to avoid the differences that arose in relation to reactions to the military strikes in 2018.

ANNEX A

Composition of the Expert Group*

Chair

Prof. Dr. Cyrille Fijnaut, Erasmus University Rotterdam, KU Leuven and Tilburg University

Members of the Expert Group

Mr. Kristian Fischer, Danish Institute for International Studies

Prof. Dr. Terry Gill, University of Amsterdam and Netherlands Defence Academy

Prof. Dr. Larissa van den Herik, Leiden University

Prof. Dr. Martti Koskenniemi, University of Helsinki

Prof. Dr. Claus Kreß, University of Cologne

Mr. Robert Serry, Former Netherlands Ambassador and United Nations Special Coordinator for the Middle East Peace Process

Ms. Monika Sie Dhian Ho, Netherlands Institute of International Relations Clingendael

Ms. Elizabeth Wilmshurst, Chatham House

Prof. Dr. Rob de Wijk, Leiden University and The Hague Centre for Strategic Studies

Secretariat

Dr. Joris Larik, Leiden University and the Stimson Center

Ms. Nienke van Heukelingen, Netherlands Institute of International Relations Clingendael

---

* The chair, the members and the secretariat participated in their personal capacity and discharged their duties independently and without instructions or consultation.

DOI:10.1163/9789004445482_006

ANNEX B

Timeline of Events

International		Netherlands
Srebrenica massacre during the Bosnian War	1995	Despite the presence of UNPROFOR's Dutch battalion (Dutchbat), Srebrenica's capture and subsequent massacre occur
Kosovo War	1999	The Netherlands takes part in NATO Operation Allied Force
The International Commission on Intervention and State Sovereignty publishes its report on "The Responsibility to Protect"	2001	
	2002	NIOD report on the Srebrenica massacre leads to the resignation of the Kok II government
Invasion of Iraq	2003	The Netherlands politically and materially supports the invasion
UN World Summit Outcome document endorses R2P principles on the basis of UN Charter	2005	
	2007	The Dutch government changes its policy guidelines to the effect that it can only politically support interstate use of force in cases where there is a legal basis in international law

 | DOI:10.1163/9789004445482_007

International		Netherlands
	2010	The Davids Committee, established by the Balkenende IV government in 2009, publishes its report on the Dutch participation in the 2003 Iraq War, concluding, *inter alia*, that there had been no adequate basis in international law for the invasion The Balkenende IV government resigns after it fails to agree on extending the Dutch participation in the NATO mission in Uruzgan (Afghanistan)
Military intervention in Libya based on United Nations Security Council Resolution 1973; NATO is widely considered to have exceeded the Security Council's mandate by having contributed to regime change in Libya	2011	The Netherlands actively takes part in the intervention
Syrian Civil War	2011–	
US, UK and France conduct air strikes against chemical weapons facilities of the Assad regime in response to the chemical weapons attack on Douma in April 2018	2018	The Dutch government expresses "understanding" (*begrip*) for the air strikes

ANNEX C

Extracts from Key UN Documents

UN CHARTER

Article 2, paragraph 4

All Members shall refrain in their international relations from the threat or use of force against the territorial integrity or political independence of any state, or in any other manner inconsistent with the Purposes of the United Nations.

Article 11

1. The General Assembly may consider the general principles of co-operation in the maintenance of international peace and security, including the principles governing disarmament and the regulation of armaments, and may make recommendations with regard to such principles to the Members or to the Security Council or to both.

2. The General Assembly may discuss any questions relating to the maintenance of international peace and security brought before it by any Member of the United Nations, or by the Security Council, or by a state which is not a Member of the United Nations in accordance with Article 35, paragraph 2, and, except as provided in Article 12, may make recommendations with regard to any such questions to the state or states concerned or to the Security Council or to both. Any such question on which action is necessary shall be referred to the Security Council by the General Assembly either before or after discussion.

3. The General Assembly may call the attention of the Security Council to situations which are likely to endanger international peace and security.

4. The powers of the General Assembly set forth in this Article shall not limit the general scope of Article 10.

Article 12

1. While the Security Council is exercising in respect of any dispute or situation the functions assigned to it in the present Charter, the General Assembly shall not make any recommendation with regard to that dispute or situation unless the Security Council so requests.

 DOI:10.1163/9789004445482_008

2. The Secretary-General, with the consent of the Security Council, shall notify the General Assembly at each session of any matters relative to the maintenance of international peace and security which are being dealt with by the Security Council and shall similarly notify the General Assembly, or the Members of the United Nations if the General Assembly is not in session, immediately the Security Council ceases to deal with such matters.

Article 24

In order to ensure prompt and effective action by the United Nations, its Members confer on the Security Council primary responsibility for the maintenance of international peace and security, and agree that in carrying out its duties under this responsibility the Security Council acts on their behalf.

In discharging these duties the Security Council shall act in accordance with the Purposes and Principles of the United Nations. The specific powers granted to the Security Council for the discharge of these duties are laid down in Chapters VI, VII, VIII, and XII.

The Security Council shall submit annual and, when necessary, special reports to the General Assembly for its consideration.

Article 39

The Security Council shall determine the existence of any threat to the peace, breach of the peace, or act of aggression and shall make recommendations, or decide what measures shall be taken in accordance with Articles 41 and 42, to maintain or restore international peace and security.

Article 42

Should the Security Council consider that measures provided for in Article 41 would be inadequate or have proved to be inadequate, it may take such action by air, sea, or land forces as may be necessary to maintain or restore international peace and security. Such action may include demonstrations, blockade, and other operations by air, sea, or land forces of Members of the United Nations.

Article 51

Nothing in the present Charter shall impair the inherent right of individual or collective self-defence if an armed attack occurs against a Member of the United Nations, until the Security Council has taken measures necessary to maintain international peace and security. Measures taken by Members in the exercise of this right of self-defence shall be immediately reported to the Security Council and shall not in any way affect the authority and responsibility of the Security Council under the present Charter to take at any time such action as it deems necessary in order to maintain or restore international peace and security.

Article 99

The Secretary-General may bring to the attention of the Security Council any matter which in his opinion may threaten the maintenance of international peace and security.

***2005 UN WORLD SUMMIT OUTCOME* (A/RES/60/1)**

Use of force under the Charter of the United Nations

77. We reiterate the obligation of all Member States to refrain in their international relations from the threat or use of force in any manner inconsistent with the Charter. We reaffirm that the purposes and principles guiding the United Nations are, inter alia, to maintain international peace and security, to develop friendly relations among nations based on respect for the principles of equal rights and self-determination of peoples and to take other appropriate measures to strengthen universal peace, and to that end we are determined to take effective collective measures for the prevention and removal of threats to the peace and for the suppression of acts of aggression or other breaches of the peace, and to bring about by peaceful means, in conformity with the principles of justice and international law, the adjustment or settlement of international disputes or situations that might lead to a breach of the peace.

78. We reiterate the importance of promoting and strengthening the multilateral process and of addressing international challenges and problems by strictly abiding by the Charter and the principles of international law, and further stress our commitment to multilateralism.

79. We reaffirm that the relevant provisions of the Charter are sufficient to address the full range of threats to international peace and security.

We further reaffirm the authority of the Security Council to mandate coercive action to maintain and restore international peace and security. We stress the importance of acting in accordance with the purposes and principles of the Charter.

80. We also reaffirm that the Security Council has primary responsibility in the maintenance of international peace and security. We also note the role of the General Assembly relating to the maintenance of international peace and security in accordance with the relevant provisions of the Charter.

…

Responsibility to protect populations from genocide, war crimes, ethnic cleansing and crimes against humanity

138. Each individual State has the responsibility to protect its populations from genocide, war crimes, ethnic cleansing and crimes against humanity. This responsibility entails the prevention of such crimes, including their incitement, through appropriate and necessary means. We accept that responsibility and will act in accordance with it. The international community should, as appropriate, encourage and help States to exercise this responsibility and support the United Nations in establishing an early warning capability.

139. The international community, through the United Nations, also has the responsibility to use appropriate diplomatic, humanitarian and other peaceful means, in accordance with Chapters VI and VIII of the Charter, to help to protect populations from genocide, war crimes, ethnic cleansing and crimes against humanity. In this context, we are prepared to take collective action, in a timely and decisive manner, through the Security Council, in accordance with the Charter, including Chapter VII, on a case-by-case basis and in cooperation with relevant regional organizations as appropriate, should peaceful means be inadequate and national authorities are manifestly failing to protect their populations from genocide, war crimes, ethnic cleansing and crimes against humanity. We stress the need for the General Assembly to continue consideration of the responsibility to protect populations from genocide, war crimes, ethnic cleansing and crimes against humanity and its implications, bearing in mind the principles of the Charter and international law. We also intend to commit ourselves, as necessary and appropriate, to helping States build capacity to protect their populations from genocide, war crimes, ethnic cleansing and crimes against humanity and to assisting those which are under stress before crises and conflicts break out.

***IMPLEMENTING THE RESPONSIBILITY TO PROTECT: ACCOUNTABILITY FOR PREVENTION*, REPORT OF THE SECRETARY-GENERAL, 10 AUGUST 2017 (A/71/1016–S/2017/556) [INTERNAL FOOTNOTES OMITTED]**

2. The international community recognizes that States have the primary responsibility to protect populations from genocide, war crimes, ethnic cleansing and crimes against humanity. We also recognize that there is a collective responsibility to encourage and assist States to fulfil their primary responsibility and to use diplomatic, humanitarian and other peaceful means, in accordance with Chapters VI and VIII of the Charter of the United Nations, to protect populations from atrocity crimes. Should peaceful means be inadequate and national authorities manifestly fail to protect their populations, Member States have stated that they are prepared to take collective action, in a timely and decisive manner, in accordance with the Charter, including Chapter VII. That was agreed when all Heads of State and Government adopted the World Summit Outcome in 2005. It has been reaffirmed many times since. The Security Council has adopted more than 50 resolutions that refer to the responsibility to protect and has reaffirmed the principle at least six times. It has reminded Governments of their primary responsibility to protect, urged national authorities to ensure accountability for violations of international human rights and humanitarian law, and has twice mandated peace operations to support host Governments to fulfil their responsibility to protect. In 2009, the General Assembly reaffirmed its intention to continue consideration of the concept (see resolution 63/308). More than 100 Member States have actively contributed to the ongoing consideration by the General Assembly of the responsibility to protect during eight informal and interactive dialogues since 2009. They have used those opportunities to clarify the principle, reaffirm their commitment to it, share experiences and lessons learned, and outline the steps needed to make the responsibility to protect a reality everywhere. The Human Rights Council has adopted more than 20 resolutions that refer to the responsibility to protect. In 2016, it called upon all Member States to work to prevent potential situations that could result in atrocity crimes and, where relevant, to address the legacy of past atrocities to prevent recurrence (see resolution 33/19).

…

5. Atrocity crimes have regional and international implications that extend well beyond national borders. The massive flows of refugees and internally displaced persons they generate create immense humanitarian and protection needs and put considerable pressure on host communities,

Governments and the international community. Such crises have often strengthened calls for action, including military intervention, to protect populations, which raise difficult political and moral questions. The human and financial costs associated with the use of force when atrocity crimes have been committed are extremely high, the prospects and consequences always uncertain. In my remarks to the Security Council on 10 January 2017, I emphasized that we spend far more time and resources responding to crises than we do on preventing them. I explained that a new approach was needed, one that brings the prevention of atrocity crimes back to the fore and that closes the gap between commitment and reality. One of the principal ways in which we can do this is by strengthening accountability and ensuring the rigorous and open scrutiny of practice, in the light of agreed principles.

RESPONSIBILITY TO PROTECT: FROM EARLY WARNING TO EARLY ACTION, REPORT OF THE SECRETARY-GENERAL, 1 JUNE 2018 (A/72/884–S/2018/525)

28. In paragraph 139 of the 2005 World Summit Outcome, the Security Council's special responsibility for the prevention of atrocity crimes was affirmed. In the past, the Council sometimes responded to situations only after atrocity crimes had been committed. It has, however, taken initiatives that contribute to early action. For example, it has increasingly invited and received briefings from my Special Adviser on the Prevention of Genocide. Initiatives such as Arria formula briefings, Council missions to conflict-affected countries, open thematic debates, situational awareness briefings and wrap-up sessions should all strengthen the Council's effectiveness in prevention efforts. The Council could consider how existing measures could be employed to prevent atrocity crimes. When risks of atrocity crimes are identified, the Council could utilize instruments at its disposal to better ascertain the situation and guide its decision-making.

…

31. The Security Council, the General Assembly and the Human Rights Council should consider ways to better utilize the tools at their disposal to strengthen international accountability for atrocity crimes.

32. States have put forward proposals for strengthening the effectiveness and transparency of the working methods of the Security Council as it responds to the threat and commission of atrocity crimes, such as those proposed by the Accountability, Coherence and Transparency Group and the Governments of France and Mexico.

…

44. While we have made political and institutional progress in our efforts to implement the responsibility to protect, we are confronting a widening gap between our responsibilities and the daily experience of vulnerable populations around the world. All too often, we fail to translate early warnings of atrocity crimes into decisive early action to prevent them. I call upon all States to back their commitments with action. In the present report, measures have been identified to improve our response and initiate programmes of work that will strengthen atrocity prevention in practice.

ANNEX D

The Dutch Position Concerning the 14 April 2018 Military Response to the Poison Gas Attack on Douma, Syria, on 7 April 2018

Background Note by Cyrille Fijnaut

 | DOI:10.1163/9789004445482_009

1. INTRODUCTION: WHY THIS NOTE?

1. In the letter of 10 December 2018 to the President of the House of Representatives, the Minister of Foreign Affairs, Stef Blok, explained why he would create an expert group: on the one hand, to examine whether certain developments necessitate a new perspective on political support for the use of force between states by other countries (not the use of force by the Netherlands itself) and, on the other hand, to investigate whether the Netherlands should push for international acceptance of humanitarian intervention as a possible new legal basis for the use of force between states in exceptional circumstances. He repeated in this letter that on 14 April 2018 the Dutch government expressed its "understanding" (*begrip*) for the response of the United States, the United Kingdom and France to the poison gas attack on Douma, Syria, and judged their response to be "proportional and well-considered" because the Netherlands believes that it is vital that the international community vigorously upholds the norm of international law that chemical weapons must never be used. The Minister equally repeated in the letter of 10 December that the Dutch government had difficulties with the statement as adopted by the North Atlantic Council (NAC) because it expressed "full support" (*volledige steun*) for the actions of the named countries, while the Netherlands did not go further than expressing "understanding" (*begrip*). In the explanation of its vote within the NAC, it stated that, despite this reservation, it voted in favour of this "full support" statement on the grounds of North Atlantic Treaty Organization (NATO) solidarity. The Netherlands was the only NATO member state to issue such an explanation of its vote.

2. In addition to this historical reference, the Minister of Foreign Affairs stated in the letter of 10 December 2018 that it was conceivable that in the near future the Netherlands will again be confronted with such a situation "in which it is asked to express political support for the use of force between states, even when there is no basis for such action in international law, as currently required by the Netherlands". In conjunction with this last observation, he added that when we – in the Netherlands – speak of a "basis" in international law, we are referring to the applicability of one of the established exceptions to the fundamental principle of international law that the use of armed force is not permitted in international relations. And in relation to these exceptions, the Minister not only refers to letters to Parliament in 2007 and 2013 but also to its response, in 2010, to the report of the Committee of Inquiry on Iraq (the Davids Committee) that the expression of political support for the use of force between states requires a basis in international law.

3. With a view to an adequate answer to the two questions that the Dutch government has formulated for the Expert Group, it is first of all necessary to elucidate within limits the background and the content of the letters published in 2007 and 2013 as well as the report of the Davids Committee and the reaction of the government to this report. Otherwise it is – for a non-Dutch audience – rather difficult to understand why it was so important for the Dutch government to distance itself to some extent from the statement that was made by the NAC and – referring to the first question – why it is looking for a new perspective on political support for the use of interstate force. In the second place, it is important – given the fact that the reaction of the Dutch government in the framework of the NAC to some extent differed from the reactions of other member states of NATO – to go into detail with regard to the positions that, in parallel with the United States, some of the closest European allies of the Netherlands (the United Kingdom, Belgium, Germany and France) not only took in the framework of NATO but also in the framework of the European Union and the United Nations. An overview of their positions – in comparison with the Dutch position – could be useful for a suitable answer in particular to the second question the Expert Group has to answer because it could generate ideas for pushing for international acceptance of humanitarian intervention as a possible new legal basis for the use of force between states in exceptional circumstances.

4. The foregoing more or less indicates the structure of this note:

   - Section II sketches in broad lines the background of the position the Netherlands took on 14 April 2018 – its position itself is outlined in section III;
   - Section IV contains an overview of the positions of its closest allies (the United States, the United Kingdom, France, Germany, and Belgium) and section V specifies the positions of NATO as well as the European Union;
   - Section VI details the confrontation that took place in the Security Council concerning the poison gas attack on Douma as well as the military response to this attack;
   - Section VII presents some comments from the academic community which specifically relate to the military response on 14 April 2018;
   - Section VIII contains some general concluding remarks.

   These contents already hint at the overarching aim of this note: to present in a descriptive manner the information that is needed with a view to the development of a grounded and balanced judgment on (the debate with regard to) the military response to the poison gas attack on Douma on 7 April 2018. This objective not only explains why a serious effort has been made in this note to refrain as much as possible from formulating comments and conclusions about this case, but also why an abundance of direct quotes from the relevant documents have been included. These quotes should enable the reader as much as possible to form his/her opinion about what has happened on 7 and 14 April 2018 and what has been said about it.

II. THE BACKGROUND TO THE DUTCH POSITION ON 14 APRIL 2018

II.1. In the Shadow of the Srebrenica Massacre

5. On 26 June 1995, just a few weeks before the mass slaughter of thousands of Bosnian Muslims in Srebrenica, the Ministers of Foreign Affairs and Defence sent a so-called Assessment Framework (*Toetsingskader*) to the House of Representatives (*Tweede Kamer*) to further the debate in the House on the dispatching of military units on behalf of international operations.[1] This framework was meant to formulate in a clear manner the way in which the government – in conformity with its constitutional duty (art. 68 of the Constitution) – had in the past cooperated with the House in this field. One of the important starting points concerned the involvement of the Netherlands in out-of-area operations (outside of NATO-territory) in order to contain a crisis. Here it was said that such operations should take place (1) in accordance with the charter of the UN, preferably on the basis of a resolution in the Security Council, and (2) either with a view to peace enforcement outside of the framework of the UN, or in order to avert large-scale and massive violations of elementary human rights in the framework of a humanitarian emergency operation.

6. In conjunction with this and other starting points, the Assessment Framework contained a number of reflections on the political desirability and the practical feasibility of participation in international operations. When it comes to political desirability – the practical feasibility is not a relevant issue in the context of this note – it is, inter alia, clearly stated that the dispatching of military units has to take place on the basis of Dutch interests (including the protection of international peace and security) and/or the advancement of the international legal order. Its advancement is not only at stake in case of operations which affect the sovereignty of countries but also gross violations of human rights, such as genocide, may constitute a reason for military intervention by the international

1 HR, 23591, no. 5, 28.6.1995.

community. However, the dispatching of Dutch military units has to be in accordance with international law and preferably should happen on the basis of a clear mandate of the United Nations or another international organization. This mandate – in the framework of the UN, preferably a resolution in the Security Council – should in general terms formulate the political and military aim of the operation.

7. On the basis of, on the one hand, an interdepartmental evaluation of the military intervention in Kosovo in 1999 and, on the other hand, a report of a special commission that evaluated the participation of the Netherlands in peace operations in the last ten years, the government again discussed with the House the political decision-making process with regard to the deployment of military units and in particular the ways in which important components of the Assessment Framework were interpreted and practically applied.

8. This debate was, however, not the only reason why the government adapted the Assessment Framework and sent a revised version in July 2001 to the House.[2] The second reason was the report that a panel of experts, under the guidance of UN ambassador Lakhdar Brahimi, published on 21 August 2000 about the ways the execution of peace operations could and should be improved. And the third reason was a change to the most relevant articles (Articles 97 and 100) of the Constitution. The most relevant article in the framework of this note is Article 100. In Article 100 (1) it is stated that the government shall inform the States General in advance if armed forces are to be deployed or made available to enforce or to promote the international legal order. This shall include the provision of humanitarian aid in the event of armed conflict. Article 100 (2) continues by saying that the provisions of paragraph 1 shall not apply if compelling reasons exist to prevent the provision of information in advance; in this event information shall be supplied as soon as possible.

9. With regard to armed humanitarian intervention, it was repeated in the revised Assessment Framework 2001 that the dispatching of military units only could take place to enforce or to promote the international legal order, including the prevention or the ending of serious and massive violations of fundamental human rights. In contrast with the 1995 version of the Assessment Framework, the revised 2001 version contained a special section on the mandate. Here it is clearly stated that the deployment of Dutch military units has to be in accordance with international law. In case the operation does not take place at the invitation of the related country, it has to be based on a clear mandate. This mandate usually

---

2 HR, 23591/26454, no. 7, 13.7.2001. See also the Davids Report, 2010, 407–409.

originates from the United Nations and in principle is in the form of a resolution in the Security Council, which should formulate the political and military ends of the operation. Furthermore, a distinction has to be made between operations for a specific period of time, as defined by the international organization, and operations which should achieve a specific aim. The mandate should also show whether it concerns an operation in the framework of chapter VI or of chapter VII of the Charter of the UN.

10. A year after the fall of Srebrenica, on 6 September 1996, the Minister of Foreign Affairs and the Minister of Defence announced their intention to instruct the Netherlands Institute for War Documentation (NIWD) to investigate events before, during and after the fall of the town.[3] The report that a research group, chaired by the director of the NIWD, Prof. Dr. Hans Blom, published on 10 April 2002 contained a number of explosive conclusions, not only for the Dutch government but for the United Nations as a whole. A few quotes from the Blom Report may illustrate the nature of these conclusions in relation to the decision-making process in the Netherlands:

- International interventions are rarely so preventive that they can be made before excesses occur. If those excesses do occur, the public debate on them often leads governments to intervene on moral and humanitarian grounds. More in-depth analysis of the background of trouble spots and measures based on such analysis rarely play a major role;
- The decision to become one of the main suppliers of troops for a peace mission moved many at the time. Dutch politics were dominated by the call to intervene on moral grounds. This humanitarian motivation, coupled with the ambition to improve Dutch credibility and prestige in the world, led the Netherlands to offer to dispatch the Air Brigade.

These and other conclusions were the reason for the Kok Cabinet resigning on 16 April 2002.[4]

11. In the meantime, on 12 October 1999, the Minister of Foreign Affairs had asked – on behalf of the government – the Advisory Council on International Affairs (ACIA) and the Advisory Committee on Issues of Public International Law (ACIPIL) to prepare a common advice on humanitarian intervention. In particular he wanted these high-level advisory bodies to pay attention to Article 39 of chapter VII of the UN Charter, which has

3 Its report (also in English) is available at http://www.srebrenica.nl.

4 In relation to the impact of the Srebrenica massacre on international law, see Ryngaert and Schrijver, 2015.

the aim to end large-scale human suffering. The reason for this particular question was that experience had shown that the Security Council is not always capable of taking timely effective measures and that in such a situation a country or a group of countries could make an attempt – without authorization by the Security Council and without the permission of the related country – to end these violations of human rights with force or the threat of force. And although such an intervention on political and moral grounds may be justified there is no clear and generally accepted legal basis for it. And the lack of such a basis carries two risks: on the one hand the abuse of the concept of humanitarian intervention for different military operations, and on the other hand the undermining of the position of international law because of the fact that it offers no possibility to intervene in the case of serious violations of generally accepted human rights. Therefore, it is very important to develop such a concept.

12. The report that the ACIA and the ACIPIL published in 2000 indeed made an effort to elucidate the concept of humanitarian intervention by making a distinction between humanitarian intervention *with* a mandate of the Security Council and humanitarian intervention *without* such a mandate.[5] In its conclusions and recommendations, they first of all stipulated that in the 1990s, for a number of reasons, an increasing tension manifested itself between, on the one hand, the prohibition of use of force between states and the respect for territorial integrity and, on the other hand, the obligation to enforce and advance human rights. Secondly, those advisory bodies concluded that the Security Council also in the future for political reasons would not be willing or would not be able to intervene with force in a humanitarian emergency situation, but that international law at that moment offered no legal basis for humanitarian intervention and that such a basis was not yet emerging. In other words, one could only acknowledge that, in general, situations exist wherein such serious and large-scale violations of human rights take place that states feel obliged to intervene with military means. If they do so, they have to justify their military intervention in the framework of the United Nations because in legal terms it still is a violation of the international legal order. Such a violation, however, is only justified when the intervening states can demonstrate that they had to act in order to prevent or to oppose a far graver infringement of that same legal order. If the permanent members of the Security Council are unable to reach agreement in such a situation, the states in question have to look for another legitimation for their intervention. This legitimation

5 Adviesraad Internationale Vraagstukken/Advisory Council on International Affairs and Commissie van Advies inzake Volkenrechtelijke Vraagstukken/Advisory Committee on Issues of Public International Law, *Humanitaire interventie/Humanitarian Intervention*, Den Haag/The Hague, April 2000.

could be acquired by taking the question to the UN General Assembly by making use of the procedure that is contained in the Uniting for Peace Resolution 1950.

13. This recommendation means that the ACIA and the ACIPIL in fact accepted – pending the further development of a justification based on international law – that in extreme cases and by way of an "emergency exit" humanitarian interventions are admissible. However, this position presupposes, the ACIA and ACIPIL emphasized, that with a view to the evaluation of such interventions a framework should be developed that contains the minimum conditions that states have to take into account and that, in addition, can structure the deliberations in the United Nations with regard to specific instances of intervention. In its opinion, such an Assessment Framework could, if strictly observed, also encourage international acceptance of a separate justification for unauthorized humanitarian intervention under international law, in which humanitarian necessity prevails over the law banning the use of force. The ACIA and the ACIPIL finally identified four key questions that need to be answered in connection with the Assessment Framework proposed here: which states may carry out a humanitarian intervention, when are states allowed to do so, what norms do the intervening states have to obey, and when and how do they have to end a humanitarian intervention? This Assessment Framework should be considered, in appropriate cases, as a minimum precondition for unauthorized humanitarian intervention.

II.2. The Impact of the War in Iraq

14. The Netherlands not only gave political support (*politieke steun*) to the US-British attack on Iraq in 2003 but was to some extent also involved "in military action in, around and over Iraq prior to and during the invasion", as the Davids Committee established. It supported the movement of sensitive military equipment on Dutch territory, stationed Patriot rockets in Turkey and contributed – after the invasion – a contingent of 1,100 military personnel to the stabilization and security force in the South of Iraq. Both issues heavily fuelled the political debate in the country with regard to the legal basis and the mandate of missions in which Dutch military units participate.[6] This explains why after years of discussion, it was said in the governmental policy statement of the Balkenende IV Cabinet dated 7 February 2007 that the Netherlands would attune its security policy to the new situation in the world and would focus on

6 See the Davids Report (Commissie-Davids), 2010, chapters 5, 6 and 8, and the summary in English.

peace missions, the fight against terrorism, prevention of conflicts, and reconstruction. This statement was immediately followed by the sentence: an adequate legal mandate is required in case of participation in missions in which Dutch military personnel is deployed; the so-called Assessment Framework constitutes the guideline for the decision-making process whereby parliamentary involvement is guaranteed. These few lines got considerable attention during the debate in the Senate on the position of the government concerning Iraq and on the meaning of the words "adequate legal mandate". In response to this debate, the government promised to prepare a note in which these words would be fleshed out in order to further the debate in both Chambers on the position that should be taken in this field.

15. On 22 June 2007, the Ministers of Foreign Affairs and Defence sent the related note to the House.[7] First of all it is stated in this note that the Assessment Framework 2001 is left completely intact. Secondly it is observed that, although a distinction should be made between the general legal basis for military missions and their mandate, it is self-evident that a mandate has to be founded on that basis. Thirdly it is emphasized that in case of a military operation in which the Dutch military is not involved, the government can only offer political support if there is a legal basis for that operation. Fourthly it is recalled that in conformity with the Assessment Framework 2001 the deployment of military units – also in case of the prevention or ending of serious and massive violations of human rights – should be in accordance with international law, i.e. in principle a resolution in the Security Council, and should be based upon a clear mandate. In the wake of these starting points the note continues by portraying the two generally accepted legal bases for interstate use of force: on the one hand individual and collective self-defence (art. 51 of the UN Charter) and on the other hand with the permission/authorization of the Security Council.[8]

16. In conjunction with this exposé, two issues are highlighted. The first one is that one cannot deduce from resolutions in the Security Council, which do not contain an explicit authorization to use force, an implicit authorization to do so. The second issue relates to the upcoming doctrine of *Responsibility to Protect* (R2P). Here it is observed – referring to the miserable situation in Darfur at the time – that a distinction has to be

---

7 HR, 29521, no. 41, 22.6.2007.

8 In relation to the response to the 9/11 attacks, the Dutch government asked the ACIA to prepare an advice on the room for self-defence before an armed attack takes place (pre-emptive strike). See Adviesraad Internationale Vraagstukken/Advisory Council on International Affairs, *Preëmptief optreden/Preemptive Action*, Den Haag/The Hague, 2004.

made between two situations. The first one concerns a situation in which the Security Council – because the right to veto has been invoked or the required majority of votes has not been attained – is not able to take decisions and the related state is not willing to execute its decisions. The second one relates to a situation in which no unanimity can be reached on a resolution in the Security Council but the international community is of the opinion that military intervention is legitimate/lawful. An example of the latter situation is a threatening humanitarian emergency situation in which the Security Council could not fulfil the principle of Responsibility to Protect.

17. In the wake of this example, the note discusses other legal bases for exceptions to the prohibition to use force. In the first order, it explains the third generally accepted legal basis for military intervention: an invitation by the country in question. In the second order – referring to what happened in Kosovo in 1999 – it elaborates upon the report of the ACIA and ACIPIL from 2000 with regard to humanitarian intervention that has already been discussed in this note, and draws the following conclusion from it: the government endorses the judgment of both bodies that in a humanitarian emergency situation a military intervention can be justified on moral and political grounds, although a clear legal basis is lacking; the lack of such a basis does not alter the fact that humanitarian intervention in extreme cases and under strict conditions by way of an emergency exit can be permissible. In conjunction with this conclusion, the government emphasizes that in such situations an ultimate effort should have been made to achieve unanimity in the Security Council on the necessity of military intervention. And it adds to this that in such situations military interventions should also be based upon principles of international law that are generally accepted. In particular the government states that even in a situation in which a veto was used in the Security Council against a resolution that would permit military intervention in relation to serious and massive violation of human rights, it may not be ruled out that ultimately military force is necessary to end a humanitarian crisis. In a discussion on such an intervention one should, however, also take into account the risks related to remaining detached or taking ineffective action. The government illustrates this position with the Srebrenica and Rwanda genocide cases and repeats that, if in the situation of genocide military intervention is necessary, it should be limited to exceptional cases because of the risks of abuse or the erosion of the prohibition of force principle and of undermining the position of the Security Council. Nevertheless one also needs to take into account the fact that in the international community the general feeling can exist that such action is lawful.

18. The Balkenende Cabinets I (2002–2003), II (2003–2006), III (2006) and IV (2007–2010) time and again opposed the establishment of an independent committee of inquiry into the policy that successive governments had pursued in relation to the war in Iraq. In February 2009, however, Prime Minster Balkenende and the Ministers of Foreign Affairs, Defence and Internal Affairs announced that a committee of inquiry, chaired by the former President of the Supreme Court, would be charged with an inquiry into the decision-making process with regard to the Dutch policy concerning Iraq in the period summer 2002 – summer 2003. One of the reasons why the Cabinet changed its position was that the political and, much more widely, the societal debate on involvement in the Iraq War had persisted. The Davids Committee presented its report on 13 January 2010. Its conclusions were relatively harsh for the government. To give an idea of the message they conveyed:

   - 4: The Dutch government's decision to take no active military part in the war against Iraq was consistent with the majority view of the Dutch public, as reflected in opinion polls of the time. The decision to express political support for the war, despite the fact that it had not been mandated by the Security Council, was inconsistent with the majority view of the Dutch public, as reflected in opinion polls;
   - 6: The Prime minister took little or no lead in debates concerning the Iraq question; he left the matter of Iraq entirely to the Minister of Foreign Affairs. Only after January 2003 did the Prime Minister take a strong interest in this issue;
   - 19 and 20: The Netherlands made it very clear that it attached great importance to a so-called "second resolution" but this position was toned down because the government consistently added that a second resolution was politically desirable, but not legally indispensable. Hence the military action had no sound mandate under international law;
   - 33: The government did not disclose to Parliament the full content of the request that the US made to the Netherlands on 15 November 2002, concerning cooperation with planning for the mobilization of a military force to compel Iraq to comply with Security Council Resolution 1441.

   A few hours after the presentation of the report Prime Minister Balkenende was questioning some of the conclusions, including conclusions 19–20, referring in particular to the dissenting observation of one of the members of the Committee, the prominent ambassador Peter van Walsum, who stated that perhaps it would have been better if before the invasion the Prime Minister had explained to the House and the Dutch people in general that there was no convincing legal basis but that a military intervention for a number of reasons was nevertheless called for. This response was not accepted by the Social-Democratic Party (*Partij van de Arbeid*), the most important coalition partner of the Christian-Democratic Party (*Christen-Democratisch Appel*). For this reason, the Prime Minister was more or less forced to write a letter to the House on behalf of the Cabinet on 9 February 2010 in which he stated that the coalition agreement – and in its wake the letter of 22 June 2007 to the House – says that participation of military units in a mission seeks an adequate legal mandate (*een adequaat volkenrechtelijk mandaat*) and that the same applies to political support (*politieke steun*) by the Netherlands in situations in which other countries undertake similar missions. He added to this that against this background and with the benefit of hindsight the Cabinet now accepted that a more adequate legal mandate (*een adequater volkenrechtelijk mandaat*) would have been necessary for the action in relation to Iraq.[9] This compromise, however, was only a sticking plaster on the already very strained relationship between the coalition partners. At the time – 23 February 2010 – they could not come to an agreement upon the request of the United States to extend the Dutch participation in the NATO mission in Afghanistan (Uruzgan), the *Partij van de Arbeid* left the coalition and the Cabinet resigned.[10]

II.3. What to do in a Case like Syria?

19. The discussion in the House on the evaluation of the Dutch contribution to the International Security Assistance Force (ISAF) in Afghanistan in February 2012 led to a letter from the Ministers of Foreign Affairs and Defence in the new Rutte II Cabinet (2012–2017), consisting of the Liberal Party (*Volkspartij voor Vrijheid en Democratie*) and the *Partij van de Arbeid*, on the effectiveness of the Assessment Framework. In their opinion this framework – that was partly revised in 2009 with a view to the development of the NATO Response Force and partly to broaden its scope in the field of developmental assistance[11] – had functioned rather well in the foregoing years and that even the increased concern with the protection of civilians in armed conflicts was no reason to change it again.[12]

---

9 HR, 31 847, no. 18, 9.2.2010.

10 On 16 February 2010 the House discussed in great detail the letter dated 9.2.2010 from the Prime Minister. See HR, TK 55, 16.2.2010.

11 HR, 30162, no. 11, 1.7.2009.

12 HR, 29521, no. 191, 9.7.2012. See also the subsequent exchange of questions and answers in HR, 29521, no. 195, 5.11.2012.

20. This conclusion was not fully in line with the recommendations in the report that the ACIA had published in 2010 on the role the Netherlands could play in the operationalization of the R2P doctrine.[13] Here it was said that it was desirable that the Netherlands would integrate this doctrine into its foreign and defence policy in the broader context of the promotion and protection of human rights and its duty under Article 90 of the Constitution to promote the development of international law. In particular the Netherlands should reflect on the way in which the Dutch contribution to a military action in the framework of R2P in accordance with the Assessment Framework could be organized, notably in relation to the use of force. In conjunction with this last observation, the ACIA also recommended that the Netherlands should further the discussion on the criteria for the use of force – with a mandate of the Security Council – in the framework of R2P, although the margins for such a development were limited. In the framework of the debate on the future of NATO, it should in any case take the position that NATO action in (the threat of) R2P situations should be possible if there is a mandate – and preferably an explicit request – from the Security Council. In its concluding remarks the ACIA emphasized that in order to prevent (the threat of) genocide more is needed than formulating a framework for action and preparing the right instruments for its use, in particular the political will to act at national and international level. How such a will could be mobilized was – the ACIA stressed – outside the scope of its advice but one should in any case take into account that it would become increasingly hard in case of (the threat of) genocide, war crimes, ethnic cleansing and crimes against humanity to justify the absence of political will to act to the media, civil society, the general public and, especially, the civilians whose rights and lives are at stake.

21. The ACIA will not have expected that shortly after the publication of the report, its final reflections would be put to the test in relation to the developments in Syria. These developments in any case urged the Minister of Foreign Affairs to write a letter to the House on 19 September 2013 concerning alternative legal mandates to intervene.[14] In this letter he explained – referring to the letter of 22 June 2007 – in a clear manner the two legal exceptions with regard to the prohibition of the use of force: self-defence and authorization by the Security Council enshrined in a

13 Adviesraad Internationale Vraagstukken/Advisory Council on International Affairs, *Nederland en de "Responsibility to Protect"; de verantwoordelijkheid om mensen te beschermen tegen massale wreedheden/The Netherlands and the "Responsibility to Protect"; The Responsibility to Protect People against Mass Atrocities*, Den Haag/The Hague, September 2010.

14 HR, 32623, no. 110, 19.9.2013.

resolution. Subsequently he stated that as a consequence of the lack of unanimity in the Security Council the use of force in Syria or other measures could not be discussed. Given this situation he wanted to elaborate on the four alternatives that had been put on the agenda in the deliberations with the House: (a) Responsibility to Protect, (b) Uniting for Peace, (c) violation of international law, and (d) humanitarian intervention:

- Option (a) was not an option in this case because the responsibility to protect without a mandate of the Security Council is no alternative legal basis for the use of force;
- Option (b) did not offer an alternative legal basis because measures that include the use of force belong to the exclusive domain of the Security Council, as has also been confirmed by the International Court;
- Option (c) as such equally did not constitute an alternative legal basis for the use of force, but the repeated use of chemical weapons is a serious violation of an imperative norm of international law and offers a basis to talk to other states on a lack of cooperation to take suitable measures, including sanctions and the use of force on the basis of a resolution in the Security Council in the framework of chapter VII of the Charter;
- Option (d) was also not an alternative legal basis at that moment.

This was of course a very unsatisfactory answer to a situation in which governments commit crimes against their people and the international community cannot offer adequate protection to the citizens concerned, but the developments in international law since 2007 did not allow for a different judgment. Nevertheless when a political judgment has to be made as to whether the use of humanitarian intervention is legitimate on the basis of a political or moral justification, one has to consider the following aspects: (a) the existence of a humanitarian emergency situation (and the repeated use of chemical weapons can constitute the basis for such a situation), (b) its existence has to be demonstrated on the basis of convincing and trustworthy evidence, it should be clear who is responsible for that violation, for example as stated in a report of the Secretary-General of the UN, and there should be no practical alternative to stop or to reduce the humanitarian emergency, and (c) the premeditated use of force should be focused on the ending or at least the reduction of the humanitarian emergency, it may never be applied as an act of retaliation or as a punitive expedition, it should meet the principles of necessity and proportionality, it should be limited in time and volume in relation to its aim, and the rules of international humanitarian law must be observed.

Besides, the Minister of Foreign Affairs in the first half of 2014 explained in several letters to the House why some limited changes to the Assessment Framework were desirable, notably in relation to military missions in which not only the enforcement or the promotion of the international legal order is at stake but also other (overlapping) aims play an important role, in particular the protection of civilians.[15] The last addition demonstrates that at this time the R2P doctrine was to some extent indeed embedded in the Assessment Framework.[16]

III. THE DUTCH POSITION CONCERNING THE MILITARY RESPONSE TO THE POISON GAS ATTACK ON DOUMA

22. On 11 April 2018 the Minister of Foreign Affairs wrote in a letter to the House that on the night of Saturday 7 – Sunday 8 April 2018, an attack took place on Douma, in Eastern Ghouta, that the first images of the attack indicated that chemical weapons had been used, that the Cabinet was of the opinion that this was probably the case, and that the Syrian regime was probably responsible for this attack with poison gas (chlorine), referring to the use of poison gas by the regime in the recent past as having been proven by the OPCW-UN Joint Investigative Mechanism.[17] In conjunction he listed the initiatives the Dutch government in the framework of the Security Council had taken in order to stop the bombardment in Syria and to start an independent inquiry into the use of chemical weapons and the identification of those who were responsible for this, but that the mandate of the Joint Investigative Mechanism in 2017 had not been extended as a result of a Russian veto and that an American proposal for a new and robust investigation mechanism had also been vetoed by Russia. A Russian proposal for an investigation wherein the Security Council itself would attribute responsibility for the use of chemical weapons received insufficient votes. The same happened to the Russian proposal to welcome the ongoing investigation by the Organization for the Prohibition of Chemical Weapons (OPCW) Fact-Finding Mission but without the power to attribute responsibility for their use.

23. A few days later, on 14 April 2018, the Minister of Foreign Affairs sent two letters to the House of Representatives.[18] In the first letter he informed

15 HR, 29521, no. 226, 22.1.2014, and no. 245, 21.5.2014.

16 Cf. the answer of the Minister of Foreign Affairs in a list of questions and answers regarding the Dutch participation in peace missions to question 20: HR, 29521, no. 245, 22.5.2014.

17 Letter dated 11.4.2018 from the Minister of Foreign Affairs to the President of the House of Representatives.

18 Letters dated 14.4. 2018 from the Minister of Foreign Affairs to the President of the House of Representatives, HR 32623, nos. 210 and 211.

the House that in response to the attack on Douma, the United States, the United Kingdom and France launched three rocket attacks on 14 April at three targets in Syria which according to these three countries were used by the Syrian regime for research, development, storage and testing of chemical weapons. He added that the Cabinet expressed understanding for this reaction that in the given circumstances was well considered and proportional. The action of the three allies, he continued, was aimed at the elimination of the capacity of the Syrian regime to use chemical weapons and in order to prevent in this way as much as possible their use in the future. The Cabinet, he further emphasized, finds it of the utmost importance that the international community stands firm in upholding the norm in international law, which states that chemical weapons never may be used. The Netherlands, he repeated, has already for a long time supported the efforts to counter the unpunished use of chemical weapons, also in the framework of the Security Council, and utterly deplores the failure of these efforts. In addition, he pointed out that the conflict in Syria cannot be solved with military means and that the Netherlands – also with a view to regional stability – dedicates itself to a credible political transition in accordance with Resolution 2254 of the Security Council. In the second letter the Minister of Foreign Affairs repeated that the Cabinet expressed its understanding for the reaction of the United States, the United Kingdom and France. In addition, he mentioned that the statement of the European Union expressed support for all efforts aiming at the prevention of the use of chemical weapons and that the North Atlantic Council (NAC) stated full support for the response of those countries. In an explanation of vote within the NAC that was officially registered in the records of the meeting, the Netherlands explained its own position, however, and made clear that it found it difficult to agree upon the statement of the NAC in which full support is expressed for the military actions, whereas the Cabinet wanted to continue to express its understanding. Out of solidarity with NATO, the Cabinet decided in the end – with this observation – to agree to the text of the statement.

24. Later that year the Minister of Foreign Affairs explained in the House the position of the Cabinet in relation to the response of the United States, the United Kingdom and France several times. He did this for the first time on 17 April 2018 on the occasion of a debate with regard to the letters of 14 April 2018, and in particular in relation to the fact that the Dutch government had expressed its understanding of that response.[19] In particular, a member of the socialist party SP (*Socialistische Partij*) asked the Minister about the facts which were the basis for this statement. His answer was

19 HR, 74th meeting, Tuesday 17 April 2018.

that the efforts of the Dutch government were of course directed at the establishment of the related facts but that the Russian vetoes with regard to the necessary joint investigation mechanism made it impossible to ascertain them. And this was, by the way, also one of the reasons why the Dutch government supported the initiative of France to prohibit the use of a veto when weapons of mass destruction had been deployed.

25. The second time the Minister clarified the Dutch position was in his answers to a number of questions that had been raised in the Permanent Committee of Foreign Affairs concerning his letters of 14 April 2018.[20] One of the questions concerned the difference between "understanding" (*begrip*) and "support" (*steun*). The answer to this question was that the Cabinet always takes into account all relevant factors in its judgment, including available intelligence, aspects of international law, circumstances, and the aim and scope of the actions. In this case the Cabinet preferred to express understanding and not political support. In relation to questions regarding the legal basis for military interventions, he referred to the letters of his predecessors from 2007 and 2013, which were presented earlier in this note. With regard to the number of times the use of chemical weapons as well as the responsibility for their use had been established, the Minister referred to the reports of the OPCW Fact-Finding Mission (with certainty or a large degree of certainty: 13 cases), the Joint Investigative Mechanism (6 cases: 4 times by the Syrian regime; twice by ISIS) and the Independent International Commission of Inquiry that in 2011 had been installed by the Human Rights Council of the United Nations (34 confirmed cases since 2013; the great majority by the Syrian regime). In addition, he reminded the members of the House of the fact that the OPCW had declared that Syria had reported that all chemical weapons, ammunition and production facilities had been destroyed when it became a Party to the Chemical Weapons Convention in 2013, but the Declaration Assessment Team of the OPCW had not yet finalized its tasks and Syria had not presented up to that moment a full overview of the scope of its chemical weapons program.

26. Finally the Minister of Foreign Affairs again elucidated in his letter to the House dated 10 December 2018 concerning the creation of an expert group to study the issues of political support for the use of force between states and humanitarian intervention, the position the Cabinet had taken on 14 April 2018 – also in the framework of the NAC – with regard to the response of the United States, the United Kingdom and France to the poison gas attack on Douma. In particular he clarified a little further – as already

20 HR, 32623, no. 221, 22.6.2018.

mentioned in the introduction to this note – the distinction between "understanding" and "support" by writing:

> "It is conceivable that in the near future the Netherlands will again be confronted with such a situation, in which it is asked to express political support for the use of force between states, even when there is no basis for such action in international law, as currently required by the Netherlands. When we speak of 'a basis in international law', we are referring to the applicability of one of the established exceptions to the fundamental principle of international law that the use of armed force is not permitted in international relations."

In other words, the Minister stated here: to express "political support" (*politieke steun*) for military action is only possible in the case of one of those exceptions. In other cases, it is only possible under certain conditions to express "understanding" (*begrip*) for such action.

IV. THE POSITION OF THE UNITED STATES, THE UNITED KINGDOM, FRANCE, GERMANY AND BELGIUM

27. On 22 April 2018, Alonso Dunkelberg *et al.* gave an overview of the reactions of a large number of states to the Syria strikes in April 2018.[21] All in all they mapped the reactions of 53 states and came to the conclusion that they can be split into three categories:

- 19 states – including Australia, Colombia, Canada, Germany, Poland and Japan – have expressed "some kind of political support (or 'understanding') for the strikes without pronouncing on their legality", including states that nod toward legal considerations but do not affirmatively state that the US-UK-France strikes are lawful;
- Another 23 states – including the Netherlands, but also Argentina, Mexico, Austria, Sweden, Indonesia, Pakistan, India, Greece and Thailand – have adopted a spectrum of stances that "neither explicitly support nor condemn the strikes". This category reflects the fact that states had a range of responses, rather than one consistent approach, to non-commitment. In some instances, it may be possible to infer from their contextual invocation of legal principles an implicit disapproval of the strikes, as a matter of law or practice, but nevertheless these states do not explicitly dismiss the strikes. At times, whether a particular state in this category has an implicit position leaning toward

21 Dunkelberg, Ingber, Pillai and Pothelet, Mapping states' reactions to the Syria strikes of April 2018, http://www.justsecurity.org/, 22 April 2018.

support or disapproval may be a matter of debate, taking into account political context, language, and nuance;

- Finally, 11 states – including Syria, Russia, China, Venezuela and South Africa – have taken a clear stand in opposition to the air strikes as illegal under international law.

However, in order to get a more detailed image of the arguments that some of the closest allies of the Netherlands – the United States, the United Kingdom, France, Germany and Belgium – used to defend (their support or understanding for) the strikes in Syria, it is important to look into more detail at the statements they made after the military intervention. Such a more detailed image facilitates a more in-depth mutual comparison of their positions.

IV.1. The Position of the United States

28. Apart from the personal statements by President Trump, the White House issued several statements in relation to the poison gas attack on Douma and the military response of the United States, the United Kingdom and France to this attack. In addition, one should not lose sight of the fact that on 21 February 2018 the White House had already issued a strong condemnation of the attacks on Eastern Ghouta and stated that "the regime's horrific attacks demonstrate an urgent need for the UN-led Geneva process to advance toward a political solution for Syria that respects the will of the Syrian people".[22]

29. On 13 April 2018 at 9:01 pm, President Trump made a statement on Syria.[23] In this statement he informed the American people that:

> "a short time ago, I ordered the United States Armed Forces to launch precision strikes on targets associated with the weapons capabilities of Syrian dictator Bashar al-Assad. A combined operation with the armed forces of France and the United Kingdom is now underway. We thank them both. Tonight, I want to speak with you about why we have taken this action. One year ago, Assad launched a savage chemical weapons attack against his own innocent people. The United States responded with 58 missile strikes that destroyed 20 percent of the Syrian air force. Last Saturday, the Assad regime again deployed chemical weapons

22 White House, Statement by the press secretary on the Syrian regime attacks on Eastern Ghouta, 21 February 2018. See in this context the analysis by Nahlawi (2015) about the so-called red line President Obama drew in 2012 with regard to the use of chemical and biological weapons by the Syrian regime.

23 White House, Statement by President Trump on Syria, 13 April 2018.

to slaughter innocent civilians – this time, in the town of Douma, near the Syrian capital of Damascus. This massacre was a significant escalation in a pattern of chemical weapons use by that very terrible regime. The evil and the despicable attack left mothers and fathers, infants and children, thrashing in pain and gasping for air. These are not the actions of a man; they are crimes of a monster instead."

In conjunction with this general starting point, he further stressed:

- "Chemical weapons are uniquely dangerous not only because they inflict gruesome suffering, but because even small amounts can unleash widespread devastation";
- "The purpose of our actions tonight is to establish a strong deterrent against the production, spread, and use of chemical weapons. Establishing this deterrent is a vital national security interest of the United States";
- "In the last century, we looked straight into the darkest places of human soul. We saw the anguish that can be unleashed and the evil that can take hold. By the end of World War I, more than one million people had been killed or injured by chemical weapons. We never want to see that ghastly specter return. So, today, the nations of Britain, France and the United States have marshaled their righteous power against barbarism and brutality."

Furthermore, the President emphasized that Assad's recent attack – and that day's response – were the direct result of Russia's failure to keep its promise to the world: they would guarantee the elimination of Syria's chemical weapons. Russia must, he continued, decide if it will continue down this dark path, or if it will join with civilized nations as a force of stability and peace.[24]

30. In parallel with this statement by the President, on 13 April 2018 the United States government published its assessment of the Assad regime's chemical weapons use.[25] This press release starts by saying that the United States:

"assesses with confidence that the Syria regime used chemical weapons in the eastern Damascus suburb of Douma on April 7, 2018, killing dozens of men, women, and children, and severely injuring hundreds more. This conclusion is based on descriptions of the attack in multiple media sources, the reported symptoms experienced by victims, videos

24 On the position of Russia, see, for example, Ferdinand, 2013, and Averre and Davies, 2015.

25 White House, United States government assessment of the Assad Regime's chemical weapons use, 13 April 2018. See also the summary in the White House press report: President Donald J. Trump has taken action to stop Syrian chemical weapons use, 13.4.2018.

> and images showing the two assessed barrel bombs from the attack, and reliable information indicating coordination between Syrian military officials before the attack. A significant body of information points to the regime using chlorine in its bombardment of Douma, while some additional information points to the regime also using the nerve agent sarin. This is not an isolated incident – the Syrian regime has a clear history of using chemical weapons even after pledging that it had given up its chemical weapons program."

Apart from a detailed overview of the precedent of the use of chemical weapons and the retention of assets, in particular the chlorine use only weeks after the use of sarin on Khan Shaykhun in April 2017 and the chemical weapons attacks (with sarin and chlorine respectively) in the Damascus area on 18 November 2017 (in the suburb of Harasta) and on 22 January 2018 (in Douma), this press release gives further details of the chemical weapons use on 7 April 2018 in the related suburb of Damascus and on the (justification of the) military response to their use:

- With a view to the empirical basis of the actions, the press report not only refers to open-source outlets, videos, images and photos, but also to the statement of the World Health Organization "about its concern over suspected chemical attacks in Syria" and to the multiple government helicopters which were observed over Douma on 7 April, with witnesses specifically identifying an Mi-8 helicopter, known to have taken off from the Syrian regime's nearby Dumayr airfield, circling over Douma during the attack. "Numerous witnesses corroborate that barrel bombs were dropped from these helicopters, a tactic used to target civilians indiscriminately throughout the war. [...] Reliable intelligence also indicates that Syrian military officials coordinated what appears to be the use of chlorine in Douma on April 7";
- The regime's continued use of chemical weapons threatens to desensitize the world to their use and proliferation, weaken prohibitions against their use, and increase the likelihood that additional states will acquire and use these weapons. To underscore this point, not only has Russia shielded the Assad regime from accountability for its chemical weapons use, but on 4 March 2018 Russia used a nerve agent in an attempted assassination in the United Kingdom, showing an uncommonly brazen disregard for the taboo against chemical weapons;
- "In this case [...] United States experts considered alternative explanations beyond the Syrian regime's culpability for chemical weapons use. [...] We have no information to suggest that this group [Jaysh al-Islam] has ever used chemical weapons, as Syria's state-run news agency has alleged. Further, it is unlikely that the opposition could

fabricate this volume of media reports on regime chemical weapons use. Such a widespread fabrication would require a highly organized and compartmented campaign to deceive multiple media outlets while evading our detection."

In the wake of this assessment, a press report of 14 April 2018 concerning the strikes in Syria states:

> "Yesterday's strikes against Syrian facilities were legitimate, proportionate, and justified. Most important, they were necessary. Chemical weapons are a unique danger to civilized nations not only because of their brutality, but because of even small amounts can trigger widespread devastation. To prevent their spread, everyone must understand that the cost of using chemical weapons will always outweigh any military or political benefits. America's past failures to act undermined that goal. With each chemical attack that goes unpunished, dangerous regimes see an opportunity to expand their arsenal. That threat alone is grave enough, but the biggest hazard is that unstable governments cannot control these stockpiles. As state inventories of nuclear, chemical, and biological weapons grow, so too does the likelihood that such weapons will fall into terrorist hands – and put American lives at risk."

In a press notice of 9 May 2018, these strikes were put into perspective: the continuation of the national emergency with respect to the actions of the government of Syria "in supporting terrorism, maintaining its then-existing occupation of Lebanon, pursuing weapons of mass destruction and missile programs, and undermining United States and international efforts with respect to the stabilization and reconstruction of Iraq".[26] Under the heading: "If the righteous many do not confront the wicked few, then evil will triumph", the strikes are depicted – in a press report of 26 September 2018 – as part of the efforts by the President in "countering the proliferation of chemical, biological, and nuclear weapons".[27]

31. On 31 May 2018, the United States Department of Justice published the *Memorandum Opinion for the Counsel to the President* on the April 2018 air strikes against Syrian chemical weapons facilities, signed by Steven Engel, Assistant Attorney General, Office of Legal Counsel.[28] This memorandum explains the bases for the conclusion that the President could lawfully

---

26 White House, Notice regarding the continuation of the national emergency with respect to the actions of the government of Syria, 9.5.2018.

27 White House, President Donald J. Trump is committed to countering the proliferation of chemical, biological, and nuclear weapons, 26.9.2018.

28 Concerning the justifications for the use of force in response to the chemical weapons attack on 6 April 2017, see Schmitt and Ford, 2017; Qureshi, 2018; Benjamin, 2018, and Henriksen, 2018.

direct those strikes "because he had reasonably determined that the use of force would be in the national interest and that the anticipated hostilities would not rise to the level of a war in the constitutional sense". As far as the first question is concerned this memorandum states that:

> "a broad set of interests would justify use of the President's Article II authority to direct military force. These interests understandably grant the President a great deal of discretion. The scope of U.S. involvement in the world, the presence of U.S. citizens across the globe, and U.S. leadership in times of conflict, crisis, and strife require that the President has wide latitude to protect American interests by responding to regional conflagrations and humanitarian catastrophes as he believes appropriate [...] We would not expect that any President would use this power without a substantial basis for believing that a proposed operation is necessary to advance important interests of the nation".

In this case the President identified three interests in support of the strikes:

> "the promotion of regional stability, the prevention of a worsening of the region's humanitarian catastrophe, and the deterrence of the use and proliferation of chemical weapons. [...] Prior to the attack, we advised that the President could reasonably rely on these national interests to authorize air strikes against particular facilities associated with Syria's chemical-weapons program without congressional authorization. [...] While the United States is not the world's policeman, as its power has grown, the breadth of its regional interests has expanded and threats to national interests posed by foreign disorder have increased."

In relation to humanitarian concerns, the *Memorandum* states that such concerns "have been a significant, or even the primary, interest served by U.S. military operations", and that "the Syrian regime's use of chemical weapons has contributed to the ongoing humanitarian crisis in Syria". Furthermore, it emphasizes that "in carrying out these strikes the President also relied on the national interest in deterring the use and proliferation of chemical weapons". And after detailing what was at stake before the strikes were carried out, the *Memorandum* concludes:

> "In sum, the President here was faced with a grave risk to regional stability, a serious and growing humanitarian disaster, and the use of weapons repeatedly condemned by the United States and other members of the international community. In such circumstances, the President could reasonably conclude that these interests provided a basis for air strikes on facilities that support the regime's use of chemical weapons."

IV.2. The Position of the United Kingdom

32. On 14 April 2018, Prime Minister Theresa May made a "Statement on Syria".[29] In this statement she said:

> "This evening I have authorized British armed forces to conduct co-ordinated and targeted strikes to degrade the Syrian Regime's chemical weapons capability and deter their use. [...] The Syrian Regime has a history of using chemical weapons against its own people in the most cruel and abhorrent way. And a significant body of information including intelligence indicates the Syrian Regime is responsible for this latest attack. This persistent pattern of behaviour must be stopped – not just to protect innocent people in Syria from the horrific deaths and casualties caused by chemical weapons but also because we cannot allow the erosion of the international norm that prevents the use of these weapons. We have sought to use every possible diplomatic channel to achieve this. But our efforts have been repeatedly thwarted. Even this week the Russians vetoed a resolution at the UN Security Council which would have established an independent investigation into the Douma attack. So there is no practicable alternative to the use of force to degrade and deter the use of chemical weapons by the Syrian Regime. This is not about intervening in a civil war. It is not about regime change. It is about a limited and targeted strike that does not further escalate tensions in the region and that does everything possible to prevent civilian casualties. And while this action is specifically about deterring the Syrian Regime, it will also send a clear signal to anyone else who believes they can use chemical weapons with impunity. [...] The speed with which we are acting is essential in co-operating with our partners to alleviate further humanitarian suffering and to maintain the vital security of our operations. [...] We cannot allow the use of chemical weapons to become normalized – within Syria, on the streets of the UK, or elsewhere else in our world. History teaches us that the international community must defend the global rules and standards that keep us all safe."

In parallel with this statement, Prime Minister's Office published a policy paper on the Syria operation: *UK Government legal position*.[30] Referring to the repeated use of chemical weapons by the Syrian regime and defining

29 GOV.UK, PM Statement on Syria: 14 April 2018, 14.4.2018 (https://www.gov.uk).

30 GOV.UK, Syria action – UK government legal position, 14.4.2018 (https://www.gov.uk/government/publications). See in this context the speech Mr. Robin Cook delivered to the American Bar Association meeting in London in July 2000 on humanitarian intervention, published in: *British Yearbook of International Law*, Oxford, Oxford University Press, 2000, 646–649. About the complicated political discussion in the United Kingdom with regard to intervention in Syria during the years 2011–2017, see Gaskarth, 2016; Kaarbo and Kenealy,

this practice as "a serious crime of international concern, as a breach of the customary international law prohibition on the use of chemical weapons, and amounts to a war crime and a crime against humanity", the paper continues as follows:

> "The UK is permitted under international law, on an exceptional basis, to take measures in order to alleviate overwhelming humanitarian suffering. The legal basis for the use of force is humanitarian intervention, which requires three conditions to be met:
>
> – There is convincing evidence, generally accepted by the international community as a whole, of extreme humanitarian distress on a large scale, requiring immediate and urgent relief;
>
> – It must be objectively clear that there is no practicable alternative to the use of force if lives are to be saved;
>
> – The proposed use of force must be necessary and proportionate to the aim of humanitarian suffering and must be strictly limited in time and in scope to this aim (i.e. the minimum necessary to achieve that end and for no other purpose).
>
> The UK considers that military action met the requirements of humanitarian intervention in the circumstances of the present case:
>
> – The Syrian regime has been using chemical weapons since 2013 [...];
>
> – Actions by the UK and its international partners to alleviate the humanitarian suffering caused by the use of chemical weapons by the Syrian regime at the UN Security Council have been repeatedly blocked by the regime's and its allies' disregard for international norms, including the international law prohibition on the use of chemical weapons. This last week, Russia vetoed yet another resolution in the Security Council, thwarting the establishment of an impartial investigative mechanism. [...] There was no practicable alternative to the truly exceptional use of force to degrade the Syrian regime's chemical weapons capability and deter their further use by the Syrian regime in order to alleviate humanitarian suffering;
>
> – In these circumstances, and as an exceptional measure on grounds of overwhelming humanitarian necessity, military intervention to strike carefully considered, specifically identified targets in order to effectively alleviate humanitarian distress by degrading

---

2016; Kaarbo and Kenealy, 2017, and Ralph, Holland and Zhekova, 2017. As far as the legal opinion as such is concerned, see Henderson, 2015.

the Syrian regime's chemical weapons capability and deterring further chemical weapons attacks was necessary and proportionate and therefore legally justifiable. Such an intervention was directed exclusively to averting a humanitarian catastrophe caused by the Syrian regime's use of chemical weapons, and the action was the minimum judged necessary for that purpose."

33. On 10 September 2018, the Foreign Affairs Committee published its Twelfth Report of Session 2017–19 on *Global Britain: the Responsibility to Protect and humanitarian intervention.*[31] As far as the air strikes in Syria are concerned, the conclusions of the Committee are:

> "Whilst noting the divisions in legal opinion around the concept of humanitarian intervention, we agree that it seems unlikely the creators of the UN Charter would have expected that the prohibition on the use of force would be applied in a way that prevented states from protecting civilian populations and stopping mass atrocities. We therefore believe that under specific circumstances, proportionate and necessary force should be available to be used as a last resort to alleviate extreme humanitarian distress at a large scale. The absence of humanitarian intervention as a final recourse could result in the paralysis of the international system and a failure to act, resulting in grave consequences for civilian populations." (p. 18)

In conjunction with this conclusion the Committee told the government that it:

> "should provide further clarification and definition in setting out the general conditions for when a humanitarian intervention can take place. The published legal opinion in relation to the April 2018 airstrikes refers, for example, to 'an exceptional basis', 'overwhelming humanitarian suffering', and 'convincing evidence', but the parameters of what these terms mean are not sufficiently clear and therefore risk being misused and misapplied, as has been argued by some in relation to the humanitarian intervention in Libya. [...] Whilst we accept that clarity is difficult in inherently complex conflict situations and that no definition will cover each and every circumstance, definitions can help to ensure that humanitarian intervention is undertaken in future for the right reasons and in the appropriate situations."

31 House of Commons, Foreign Affairs Committee, *Global Britain: the Responsibility to Protect and humanitarian intervention*, HC 1005, Published on 10 September 2018. See further R. Ware, *The legal basis for air strikes against Syrian government targets*, House of Commons Library, Briefing paper, no. 8287, 16.4.2018.

In relation to the applicability of R2P to the Syrian conflict, the Committee takes, inter alia, the viewpoint:

> "that the UNSC is the right authority to mandate collective use of force. However, we believe that the P5 states, in holding a right to veto, have a responsibility to ensure that the narrow interests of the few do not stand in the way of protecting the many. It is an abuse of the moral responsibility entrusted to the permanent Security Council members to block action sought to prevent or alleviate suffering from mass atrocities."

Finally the Committee states that the failure to protect civilians and to prevent mass atrocities in Syria "derives principally not from the actions taken by the international community but inaction" (the price of inaction).

34. The government reacted to the report on 8 November 2018.[32] As far as the air strikes in Syria are concerned it responded to the relevant question as follows:

> "The UK's long-standing position on humanitarian intervention is that it is consistent with international law if the following three conditions are met:
>
> (i) There is convincing evidence, generally accepted by the international community as a whole, of extreme humanitarian distress on a large scale, requiring immediate and urgent relief;
>
> (ii) It must be objectively clear that there is no practicable alternative to the use of force if lives are to be saved; and
>
> (iii) The proposed use of force must be necessary and proportionate to the aim of relief of humanitarian need and must be strictly limited in time and scope to this aim (i.e. the minimum necessary to achieve that end and for no other purpose)."

The explanation with regard to these three criteria ran as follows:

- Ad (i): The circumstances must be truly exceptional for the criteria to be satisfied. The first criterion is "a very high threshold. This can be evidenced by the examples where the United Kingdom has previously intervened", e.g. in Kosovo in 1999;
- Ad (ii): "The use of force will always be an act of last resort. We first need to focus on prevention and capacity-building. We need to consider whether we can prevent atrocities by non-military means – through

32 House of Commons, Foreign Affairs Committee, *Global Britain: the Responsibility to Protect and humanitarian intervention: government response to the Committee's twelfth report*, Fifteenth Special report, Appendix.

measures short of the use of force. Humanitarian intervention will only be considered where it is necessary to safeguard a population against grave and imminent peril and where there is no other legal basis for the use of force, such as self-defence, a Chapter VII UN Security Council resolution authorizing force or host-state consent"; and

- Ad (iii): "The necessity and proportionality criterion acts as a powerful brake on any use of force, and ensures that any action is the minimum judged necessary."

"The consequence of advocating *against* humanitarian intervention is that it would be unlawful to take action to save lives where the UN Security Council is blocked from acting. That is the inevitable logical consequence of the view that international law does not permit targeted military intervention in situations of extreme humanitarian distress. [...] It is important to note that the legal basis for the intervention in Libya, contrary to the Committee's inference, was not humanitarian intervention."

In conjunction with this assessment, the response continues by stating that the United Kingdom fully supports the principle that as a matter relating to international peace and security, "the UN Security Council should be empowered to act to stop mass atrocities". That is why the United Kingdom signed up to the Accountability, Coherence and Transparency (ACT) Group's Code of Conduct in 2015, which calls on all Security Council members not to vote against a credible draft resolution on timely and decisive action to end, or prevent, the commission of genocide, crimes against humanity or war crimes.

IV.3. The Position of France

35. In a press statement dated 14 April 2018, the President of the French Republic informed the nation (also in English) of the intervention of the French armed forces in response to the use of chemical weapons in Syria.[33] This statement first of all refers to the use of chemical weapons in Douma on Saturday 7 April in "total violation of international law and United Nations Security resolutions". Secondly it is emphasized that there is "no doubt as to the facts and to the responsibility of the Syrian regime". And thirdly it said that "the red line declared by France in May 2017 has been crossed" and that therefore the armed forces received the order to intervene as part of an international operation:

33 Press statement by the President of the French Republic on the intervention of the French armed forces in response to the use of chemical weapons in Syria, *Actualités*, 14.4.2018.

"against the clandestine chemical weapons arsenal of the Syrian regime. Our response has been limited to the Syrian regime's facilities enabling the production and employment of chemical weapons. We cannot tolerate the normalization of the employment of chemical weapons, which is an immediate danger to the Syrian people and to our collective security. […] France and its partners will today continue their efforts at the United Nations to enable the creation of an international mechanism to establish responsibility, prevent impunity and obstruct any temptation on the part of the Syrian regime to repeat these acts."

Furthermore, it is said that France's priorities in Syria since May 2017 have been the fight against Daesh, humanitarian assistance to civilian populations and "triggering collective momentum to bring about a peaceful settlement of the conflict so that peace can return to Syria and to ensure the region's stability".

36. Two days later, on 16 April 2018, the Prime Minister Edouard Philippe made a lengthy statement about the French intervention in Syria in the *Assemblée nationale*.[34] In this declaration he mentioned, inter alia, that the operation of the French, American and British forces had been a success: the three relevant sites which had been selected were destroyed, and that the government had continuously updated the Parliament about the initiative.[35] In relation to the explanation and justification of the intervention, he emphasized:

- That the political and military action in the Levant would be completely in vain and the foreign policy of France completely without substance if a weapon of terror, banned by the international community nearly one century ago, could maintain barbarism against civilian populations, promote hate, undermine every possibility for a political solution, in other words contradict all the rules which human beings have developed for themselves;
- That it would be possible to find a political solution for the conflict but that no political solution can be found as long as the use of chemical weapons remain unpunished. Civilian populations pay the price of inaction. Our security itself, in France and in Europe, is at stake here. That is the reason why the President has in a clear manner drawn a red line, right from the start of his mandate;

34 Premier ministre, Déclaration de M. Edouard Philippe, Premier ministre, sur l'intervention des armées françaises en réponse à l'emploi d'armes chimiques en Syrie, 16.4.2018 (translation by CF). See in this context the analysis by Stavridis (2016) of the position of the French Parliament towards the conflicts in Libya and Syria.

35 Concerning the Franco-British military cooperation in general, see Gramyk, 2014.

- That chemical weapons have been banned from military operations since 1925 and that under the impetus of France the Chemical Weapons Convention has been signed here in Paris in 1993. At this moment, 192 states are Party to this Convention. This shows that the community of states agrees upon the prohibition of those weapons because they constitute the instrument of a war crime and affect combatants as well as civilians. Their use does not amount to a dirty war anymore but creates apocalyptic scenes. These weapons persistently shake reason and civilization;

- That not only information that has been gathered by France and its allies but also the information collected by the World Health Organization show that a chemical attack took place and that the Syrian military forces are responsible for this operation. It is the tactical manifestation of a strategy of terror that also was applied on 4 April 2017 in Khan Shaykhun. Before we decided to make use of force we did – politically and diplomatically speaking – everything possible to bring Damascus to reason;

- That France is very much devoted to multilateral cooperation but to a multilateral cooperation that is effective, but that in this case one state made it impossible to operate in a collective manner: Russia. This state used its veto 12 times last week to block the re-establishment of an independent mechanism to investigate cases in which chemical weapons have been used and to attribute responsibility for their use. Besides one may not lose sight of the fact in this context that the Security Council was already prepared to take coercive measures based on Chapter VII of the Charter. One may refer here in particular to Resolution 2118 of 27 September 2013 concerning the unauthorized transport or use of chemical weapons in Syria. It states that the Security Council, if this resolution is not respected, will take measures pursuant to Chapter VII. That is to say: France took its responsibility. In the near future our political policy will be clear and will not change;

- That the response by France was fully justified. It was designed in a proportionate manner: only directed at establishments linked to the chemical program and only directed at Syrian targets, also in order to prevent harming civilians and to prevent any escalation. So, we sent a robust and clear message and want to discourage the regime from the use of the chemical weapons while the fighting continues and the regime is in no way demonstrating a willingness to seek a political exit strategy. We want to say that no military victory can be achieved without impunity through the use of chemical weapons. Our common action aimed at maximizing the costs of the use of chemical weapons and at reducing the capacity to use such weapons by the destruction of the establishments for their production, their assembly and their storage;

- That the military has executed this operation with sang-froid and in a professional manner, and by showing its strength and the depth of its force has confirmed the status of France as a political and military power. Nevertheless, this operation was not a prelude to war because we only attacked the chemical capacities of the regime and not the allies of the regime, despite our divergent perspectives. It is also important to emphasize that the action at the international level has been widely supported, not only by our allies but also by large international organizations;
- That last Saturday the Security Council massively rejected – with 8 votes against and 4 abstentions – the Russian initiative to condemn the action. This means that the great majority of the Security Council does not support the thesis that our action would be contrary to international legality (*contraire à la légalité internationale*). Besides, in the eyes of all, it testifies to our autonomy in taking decisions;
- That history has shown that the postponement of the use of force in the face of unacceptable developments often creates an illusionary rest but that later on one has to pay a heavy cost. The use of force, however, comes down to a serious decision, because action brings risk, has a cost, a human cost and a political cost, but the government was of the opinion that the risk and the cost of inaction would be far greater yet. Greater for our future, greater also for our conscience and equally for the trace that we leave on history and in the eyes of our children. The decision taken by the President was difficult, legitimate and necessary.

37. The debate in the *Assemblée nationale* on this declaration by the Prime Minister was unsurprising.[36]

    - The political parties that supported the government readily agreed with the statement he made. One of the remarkable observations on the part of the lead representative of the political movement of the President (*La République en marche*), Richard Ferrand, was that in his opinion three resolutions in the Security Council with regard to the chemical weapons in Syria (Resolutions 2254, 2118 and 2104) fully constituted a basis for the action that had been taken. And incidentally: in cases like this one – when parents and children are being killed with gas – one should not close one's eyes and hide behind international law but one

36 Assemblée nationale, Compte rendu intégral 1re séance de lundi 16 avril 2018, No. 38, 17.4.2018.

should act. The power of France makes it possible to have human law respected (*La puissance de la France lui permet de faire respecter le droit humain*);

- The representative of the main opposition party (*Les Républicains*), Christian Jacob, was quite critical, however. He stated that the Republic in its decision to come into action without a mandate of the Security Council, crossed the precious line that his predecessors had built up in order to guarantee the independence of France. It could be that action was an operational success but this did not say anything of its political success in the long run;
- The representative of the *Mouvement démocrate*, Marc Fesneau, defended the decision of the government, saying, inter alia, that, given the Russian blockade in the Security Council, France and its allies had taken their responsibility with all the legitimacy it asks for (*avec toute la légitimité requise*). And he added that inaction meant that one condemned oneself to be a passive spectator of barbaric actions and to legitimize them in a certain way. No democrat could accept that international law and the most elementary respect for civilian populations were taunted in this way.

IV.4. The Position of Germany

38. On 14 April 2018, the federal government (*Bundesregierung*) issued a press report: *Bundeskanzlerin Merkel zu den Militärschlagen der USA, Großbritanniens und Frankreichs in Syrien*. This report refers to the use of chemical weapons in Douma and adds to this not only that the available information points to the responsibility of the Assad regime that in the past has frequently used chemical weapons against its own people, but also that Russia again by its blockade in the Security Council has prevented an independent investigation of the events. Against this background, the report continues, "our American, British and French Allies today launched targeted air strikes against military establishments of the Syrian regime, with the aim to reduce the capacity of the regime to use chemical weapons and to deter further violations of the Chemical Weapons Convention". The report goes on to say:

> "We support [*unterstützen*] the fact that our Allies as permanent members of the Security Council have taken responsibility in this way. The military intervention was needed and appropriate [*erforderlich und angemessen*] in order to guarantee the working of international respect in relation to the use of chemical weapons and to warn the Syrian regime in relation to further violations. One hundred years after

the end of the First World War all of us have the duty to counter the erosion of the Chemical Weapons Convention. Germany will resolutely support all diplomatic steps in this direction."[37]

39. In conjunction with this press statement, the German government clarified its position on 19 July 2018 in its answer to a question by some members of the *Bundestag* and the group The Left (*Die Linke*) concerning the assessment of the air strikes by the United States, France and the United Kingdom in Syria on 14 April 2018 from a viewpoint of international law.[38] The government answered the question as follows:

- Taking into account the inaction of the Security Council with regard to the serious violation of international law (*schwere Völkerrechtsverletzung*) the government assesses the action, that was a targeted one and that only was directed against establishments which are related to the use of chemical weapons, as necessary and appropriate (*erforderlich und angemessen*):
- The question as to whether there exists – apart from self-defence and authorization – also an unwritten exception (*ungeschriebenen Ausnahmetatbestand*) to the prohibition of the use of force, is from an international law viewpoint a controversial one;
- Germany supports the idea that the permanent members of the Security Council themselves on their own initiative should limit the use of the veto (*Selbstbeschränkung des Vetos*) in case of prevention or retribution (*Verhinderung und Ahndung*) of violations of international law which can be assessed as war crimes (*Kriegsverbrechen*);
- Although Russia had guaranteed the security of the members of the OPCW Fact-Finding Mission who wanted to investigate what happened in Douma on 7 April 2018, they came under fire on 17 April 2018. As a consequence of this the Mission could only start its investigation on the ground after considerable delay.

37 Die Bundesregierung, Bundeskanzlerin Merkel zu den Militärschlagen der USA, Großbritanniens und Frankreichs in Syrien, *Pressemitteilung*, 14.4.2018. See in this context also the anonymous notice by the *Wissenschaftliche Dienste* of the *Deutscher Bundestag* concerning *Völkerrechtliche Grundlagen der humanitären Hilfe unter besonderer Berücksichtigung Syriens* (Berlin, 2016) and the notice by this support service on the *Rechtsfragen einer etwaigen Beteiligung der Bundeswehr an möglichen Militärschlägen der Alliierten gegen das Assad-Regime in Syrien* (Berlin, 2018).

38 Deutscher Bundestag, *Völkerrechtliche Beurteilung der Luftangriffe seitens der USA, Frankreich und Großbritannien auf Syrien am 14. April 2018, Antwort der Regierung*, Drucksache 19/3512, 19.7.2018.

On 6 November 2018, the German government answered a parliamentary question regarding the use of chemical weapons in Syria and the ways in which their use in a number of cases had been established by the related bodies.[39]

IV.5. The Position of Belgium

40. The Ministers of Foreign Affairs and Defence, Didier Reynders and Steven Vandeput, stated in the framework of a visit to Belgium by the Director-General of the OPCW, Ahmet Üzümcü, on 7 March 2018, that Belgium condemns the use of chemical weapons by the regime and the rebel groups in Syria. Their use constitutes a war crime that should be punished. And Minister Reynders called upon the Syrian regime to create clarity to the OPCW with regard to its chemical weapons program.[40] After the attacks by the United States, the United Kingdom and France, the Prime Minister Charles Michel tweeted on the morning of 14 April 2018:

> "Belgium strongly condemns the use of chemical weapons in Syria. We show understanding for joint action of US, France and UK. Focus needs to be on political negotiations now in order to avoid escalation."[41]

In its official declaration the Belgian government repeated its condemnation of the use of chemical weapons because it amounts to a flagrant violation of international law. "Our country understands [*begrijpt*] the military action of our American, French and British partners in Syria. Their targets were the production facilities they identified. Belgium deplores the ongoing blockade in the Security Council."[42]

V. THE POSITION OF NATO AND THE EU

V.1. The Position of NATO

41. In the statement dated 14 April 2018 by the North Atlantic Council on actions taken against the use of chemical weapons in Syria, it is said that the United States, France and the United Kingdom briefed allies on their joint military action on 14 April and informed them that a significant body of information indicated that the Syrian regime was responsible for the

---

39 Deutscher Bundestag, *Einsatz chemischer Kampfstoffe in Syrien, Antwort der Bundesregierung*, Drucksache 19/5517, 6.11.2018.

40 Ministerie van Buitenlandse Zaken, België steunt strijd tegen gebruik van chemische wapens, *Newsroom*, 7.3.2018.

41 This message dated 14.4.2018 at 09.56 hrs was published by the press agency BELGA on 14 April 2018.

42 Ministerie van Buitenlandse Zaken, Syrië: Belgische verklaring, *Newsroom*, 14.4.2018.

attack against civilians in Douma on 7 April, and that their military action was limited to the Syrian regime's facilities enabling the production and employment of chemical weapons.[43] The three allies emphasized, the statement continues, that there was no practicable alternative to the use of force. As far as support for the joint military action is concerned, the statement said:

> "Allies expressed their full support for this action intended to degrade the Syrian regime's chemical weapons capability and deter further chemical weapon attacks against the people of Syria. Chemical weapons cannot be used with impunity or become normalized. They are an immediate danger to the Syrian people and to our collective security. Allies regret that the mandate of the Joint Investigative Mechanism, established by UNSC Resolution 2235 (2015), to identify perpetrators of chemical attacks, was not renewed in November 2017. Allies support international mechanism to establish responsibility and prevent impunity for the use of chemical weapons. Allies strongly condemned the repeated use of chemical weapons by the Syrian regime, and called for those responsible to be held to account. Allies also called on the Syrian regime and its backers to allow rapid, sustained and unhindered humanitarian access."

This statement was repeated in a press point by NATO Secretary-General Jens Stoltenberg after the meeting on Syria.[44]

V.2. The Position of the EU

42. In a declaration on the strikes in Syria, the High Representative Federica Mogherini stated on behalf of the European Union (EU) that the EU reiterated its strongest condemnation of the repeated use of chemical weapons by the Syrian regime, as confirmed by the OPCW-UN Joint Investigative Mechanism and as reported continuously in recent months in Eastern Ghouta and other areas in Syria, including the most recent reports of a devastating chemical attack on Douma.[45] In this context the EU was informed, the declaration continues, about targeted US, French and UK air strikes on chemical weapons facilities in Syria, these specific measures having been taken with the sole objective to prevent further use of chemical weapons and chemical substances as weapons by the Syrian

---

43 NATO, Statement by the North Atlantic Council on actions taken against the use of chemical weapons in Syria, *Newsroom*, 14.4.2018.

44 NATO, *Press point*, 14.4.2018, updated 16.4.2018. For an analysis of the discourse of the NATO Secretaries General over the years, see Alkopher, 2016.

45 Council of the EU, *Press release* 196/18, 14.4.2018.

regime to kill its own people. In relation to the support for the strikes, the statement says:

> "The EU is supportive of all efforts aimed at the prevention of the use of chemical weapons. It finds it deeply shocking that the international community is still confronted with the use of chemical weapons, as confirmed by the OPCW Fact-Finding Mission. The reports of the Declaration Assessment Team show that the Syrian declaration cannot be fully verified as accurate and complete in accordance with the Chemical Weapons Convention. Accountability is a must. The use of chemical weapons or chemical substances as weapons is a war crime and a crime against humanity. Perpetrators will be held accountable for this violation of international law. Therefore, the EU deeply regrets that the mandate of the Joint Investigative Mechanism, established by the UNSC Resolution 2235 (2015) to identify perpetrators of chemical attacks, has not been renewed in November 2017. In this respect, it is highly regrettable that the UN Security Council has so far failed to adopt a strong resolution re-establishing an independent attribution mechanism to ensure accountability for perpetrators of chemical weapons' attacks in Syria."

The official conclusions of the Council dated 16 April 2018 on Syria largely reiterated the statement of the High Representative, stating, inter alia:

> "We strongly condemn the continued and repeated use of chemical weapons by the regime in Syria, including the latest attack on Douma, which is a grave breach of international law and an affront to human decency. In this context, the Council understands that the targeted US, French and UK airstrikes on chemical weapon facilities in Syria were specific measures having been taken with the sole objective to prevent further use of chemical weapons and chemical substances as weapons by the Syrian regime to kill its own people. The Council is supportive of all efforts aimed at the prevention of the use of chemical weapons. This is the position on behalf of the EU at the OPCW."[46]

The President of the European Commission, Jean-Claude Juncker, was rather more outspoken:[47]

> "The use of chemical weapons is unacceptable in any circumstances and must be condemned in the strongest terms. The international community has the responsibility to identify and hold accountable those responsible of any attack with chemical weapons. [...] This

46 Council, MAMA 59, 7956/18, 16.4.2018.

47 This overview is based on M. Banks and J. Levy-Abegnoli, EU leaders react to Syria air strikes, *The Parliament*, 16.4.2018.

> was not the first time that the Syrian regime used chemical weapons against civilians but it must be the last. Syria desperately needs a lasting ceasefire respected by all parties that paves the way for achieving a negotiated political solution through the United Nations-led Geneva process, to bring peace to the country once and for all. After the suffering they have endured, Syrians deserve nothing less."

European Council President Donald Tusk remarked: "The EU will stand with our allies on the side of justice."

43. The largest political groups in the European Parliament reacted in similar ways. EPP group leader Manfred Weber tweeted: "I fully understand the response by US, France and UK in Syria". S&D group chair Udo Bullmann stated: "The use of chemical weapons is completely unacceptable. Now that we have seen military reaction from the US, France and the UK, we call for all countries and parties involved to de-escalate the situation and give the UN the opportunity to take up its role, to bring to an end the Syrian civil and proxy war and bring those responsible for crimes against humanity to justice." The leader of the ALDE group, Guy Verhofstadt, said: "Targeted US, France UK strikes were unavoidable. Assad must understand he cannot use chemical weapons with impunity. The international community must now lead a more systematic effort to bring peace, political transition and accountability to Syria." The co-chairs of the Green/EFA group, Ska Keller and Philippe Lamberts, said, however: "Single-handed action by the US, France and Great Britain will not end the civil war in Syria and is dangerous. It could bring down the shaky international legal order. The US President risks causing a wildfire and military escalation among the nuclear powers with his ill-considered statements. The European Union must develop a political strategy. The accounts of those responsible for the use of toxic gases must be frozen and further non-military coercive measures must not be taboo."

VI. THE CONFRONTATION IN THE SECURITY COUNCIL

44. Since 2012 the literature concerning the debate on humanitarian intervention in Syria at the level of the United Nations, and in particular within the Security Council, has mushroomed. This is easy to understand because Syria, unfortunately, constitutes the most important hard contemporary test case for theories with regard to this type of cross-border state intervention.[48] It almost goes without saying that it is in the framework of this note not possible to reconstruct that debate to the fullest. In line with

48 See Edwards and Cacciatori, 2018; Erameh, 2017; Lagerwall, 2018; Melling and Dennett, 2018; Sarvarian, 2016, and Stahn, 2013.

the foregoing presentation of the debate at the level of the most relevant allies, NATO and the EU, the presentation of the debate at the level of the United Nations in this paragraph is limited to the most crucial elements of the debate concerning the poison gas attack on Douma on 7 April 2018 and the military response by the United States, the United Kingdom and France to that attack on 14 April 2018. To further the understanding of the sharp political confrontation that in those days took place at UN headquarters, it is important to know that a few weeks earlier – on 24 February 2018 – the Security Council adopted Resolution 2401 (2018), inter alia: *demanding* all parties to cease hostilities without delay; *reiterating* the demand, reminding in particular the Syrian authorities, that all parties immediately comply with their obligations under international law, including international human rights law, as applicable, and international humanitarian law; *calling upon* all parties to immediately lift the sieges of populated areas, including in Eastern Ghouta, Yarmouk, Foua and Kefraya; and *demanding* that all parties allow the delivery of humanitarian assistance, including medical assistance, ceasing depriving civilians of food and medicine indispensable to their survival.[49]

VI.1. The Vetoed (Draft) Resolutions of 10 April 2018

45. On 10 April 2018 the Press Service of the Security Council issued a report saying that:

> "The Security Council, voting today on three separate draft resolutions in response to recent allegations of a chemical weapons attack in the Syrian town of Douma, failed to rally the votes needed to launch an 'independent mechanism of investigation' into the incident, as delegates voiced frustration over the continued paralysis and the expanding rifts between nations".[50]

The first draft resolution, submitted by the United States, requested the Secretary-General to submit recommendations about the mechanism, including its terms of reference. This draft resolution requested the Secretary-General to submit to the Security Council recommendations regarding the establishment and operation of the United Nations Independent Mechanism of Investigation (UNIMI), "based on the principles of impartiality, independence and professionalism, to identify to the greatest extent feasible, individuals, entities, groups, or governments who were perpetrators, organizers, sponsors or otherwise involved in the use of chemical weapons, including chlorine or any other chemical" in Syria.

49 Security Council, Resolution 2401 (2018), S/res/2401 (2018), 24.2.2018.
50 United Nations, Meetings coverage, SC/13288, 10.4.2018.

This draft resolution was not adopted, following a vote of 12 in favour to 2 against (Bolivia, Russian Federation) and 1 abstention (China) owing to a veto by the Russian Federation.[51]

The second, competing, draft resolution was submitted by the Russian Federation, but was rejected by a recorded vote of 6 in favour (including Bolivia, China and the Russian Federation) to 7 against (including France, the Netherlands, Poland, Sweden, the United States and the United Kingdom) with 2 abstentions (Côte d'Ivoire, Kuwait). By the terms of this text, the Council would have established a UNIMI "to identify beyond reasonable doubt facts which may lead to the attribution by the Security Council of the involvement in the use of chemicals as weapons, including chlorine or any other toxic chemical" in Syria. The draft resolution also urged the UNIMI "to fully ensure a truly impartial, independent, professional and credible way to conduct its investigations on the basis of credible, verified and corroborated evidence".[52]

One of the main differences between these two draft resolutions of course concerns the extent to which the UNIMI itself would dispose of the competence to establish the responsibility for the use of chemical weapons.

The third draft resolution was again tabled by the Russian Federation and did not contain a proposal to establish an independent mechanism of investigation but asked the Council to reiterate its condemnation in the strongest terms of any use of any toxic chemical as a weapon in Syria, to express its alarm at the allegations of use of such substances in Douma on 7 April, and to express its full support to the OPCW Fact-Finding Mission. This draft resolution was equally not adopted by a vote of 5 in favour (including Bolivia, China and the Russian Federation) to 4 against (France, the United Kingdom, the United States and Poland) with 6 abstentions (including Kuwait, the Netherlands and Sweden).[53]

46. In a related meeting of the Council, the representative of the Netherlands, Karel Van Oosterom, noted that his delegation had supported the United States draft and expressed extreme disappointment that an attempt to set up an effective mechanism had failed again. If the Russian Federation thought that alleged chemical weapons attacks were fabrications, he said, then it should not have used its veto. The Netherlands would vote against

51 Security Council, Draft Resolution, S/2018/321, 10.4.2018.

52 Security Council, Draft Resolution, S/2018/175, 10.4.2018. As far as the position of Russia with regard to intervention in Syria since 2012 is concerned, see Averre and Davies, 2015; Ferdinand, 2013, and Odeyemi, 2016.

53 Security Council, Draft Resolution, S/2018/322, 10.4.2018.

the Russian draft, which fell short in every possible way: "Impunity must not prevail."

The following references to the statements of the representatives of its closest allies sufficiently illustrate their position:

- United States (Nikki Haley): the draft resolution that the United States sponsored called for unfettered humanitarian access and created the independent mechanism of investigation to determinate accountability. The one submitted by the Russian Federation gave itself the chance to choose its investigators and help determine the outcome of the investigation;
- France (François Delattre): allegations of recent attacks in Douma by the Syrian regime could constitute war crimes, stressing that, to allow such assaults would "let the genie of chemical weapons use out of the bottle" and pose an existential threat to all people. The American draft would provide a mandate for an independent mechanism of investigation to assign responsibility for the Douma attacks, stressing that only that combination of specific mandates would effectively act as a deterrent;
- United Kingdom (Karen Pierce): it was a sad day for the people of Douma, who now had no protection of the international community. With its veto, the Russian Federation had crossed a line and history was repeating itself a year after the events in Khan Shaykhun. Last autumn the Russian Federation had vetoed a renewal of the mandate of the Joint Investigative Mechanism on three occasions because it preferred to cross a line on weapons of mass destruction than risk the sanctioning of Syria.

The representative of the Russian Federation (Vassily Nebenzia) said, inter alia, that the United States was attempting to mislead the international community. The draft would have been an attempt to "recreate the Joint Investigative Mechanism – whose mandate had not been renewed in late 2017 – which had become a puppet of anti-Damascus forces and shamed itself by rendering a guilty verdict against a sovereign State with no evidence". Visits to incident sites and protecting the chain of evidence must be working principles, while the Council could determine – on the basis of reliable evidence – who was responsible for using chemical weapons. Nothing along those lines was contained in the United States draft.

VI.2. 13 April: The Warning by the Secretary-General

47. In the meeting of the Security Council on 13 April 2018, the Secretary-General said that in an 11 April letter to the Council he had expressed his deep disappointment that it was unable to agree upon a dedicated mechanism to attribute responsibility for the use of chemical weapons in Syria following the end of the mandate of the UN–OPCW Joint Investigative Mechanism. Norms against chemical weapons must be upheld, as a lack of accountability would embolden those using such arsenals by reassuring them of impunity, weakening current norms and the international disarmament and non-proliferation regime. "Increasing tensions and the inability to reach a compromise in establishment of an accountability mechanism threaten to lead to a full-blown military escalation. This is exactly the risk we face today, that things spiral out of control. It is our common duty to stop it."[54]

The representative of the Russian Federation recalled in this meeting that the United States had, on 11 April, threatened to strike Syria and stated that such an attack against a sovereign state would constitute a violation of international law and run counter to the Charter and could "not be allowed to happen". Any state daring to encroach on the principles of sovereignty and territorial integrity was unworthy of the status of a permanent member of the Council. However, one such member continued to insist on plunging the Middle East into one conflict after another. Syrian armed forces had already received instructions on how to respond to such an attack, he said, adding that there was no evidence backing up the justification being invoked by Western states – namely, the allegation of chemical weapons use in the town of Douma. The Syrian government had strongly rejected those allegations, calling on the OPCW to promptly investigate.

The representative of the United States said the emergency meeting had been convened under strange circumstances whereby the Russian Federation had asked to address "unilateral threats" while ignoring its own unilateral actions in the region. What should really be considered was the blatant violation of international law, in particular the Chemical Weapons Convention, with the use of chlorine, mustard gas and other chemical weapons. In this context the Council should not condemn the country or group of countries that had the courage to stand up for the Convention principles. Instead, it should focus on those who exhibited unilateralism in defence of chemical weapons use. Indeed, it was the Russian Federation

---

54 Security Council, Secretary-General warns Security Council to swiftly unite on Syrian conflict, preventing dangerous developments from worsening, SC/13293, 13.4.2018.

alone that had consistently defended the Assad regime, having used its veto six times to do so. While the President had not yet made up his mind on whether to act in Syria, if he and his allies chose to do so, it would be in defence of international norms.

48. In conjunction with the last statement, the representative of France said, inter alia, that the threat to international peace and security was related to the systematic use of chemical weapons by the Assad regime and that there was no doubt that Damascus was responsible for that. The successive Russian vetoes, however, had paralysed and sacrificed the Council's ability to act. The chemical weapon attack on Douma called for a robust and united response. Emphasizing France's commitment to ending impunity, he said the prohibition of chemical weapons must be restored and Damascus must not be allowed to transgress the norms of international law. The representative of the United Kingdom said that the Assad regime, with a track record of using chemical weapons, was highly likely responsible for the Douma attack. The use of chemical weapons must be challenged and the United Kingdom would work with its allies to coordinate an international response. What had occurred in Syria was a violation of the Charter and to stand by and ignore the need for justice and accountability was to place the security of all at the mercy of a Russian veto. The international order must not be sacrificed for the Russian Federation's desire to protect its ally at all costs.

49. On behalf of the Netherlands, van Oosterom said that while the Russian Federation was busy covering up the crimes of its ally, people around the world were appalled by the types of violence perpetrated by the Syrian regime. Accountability for chemical weapons use in Syria was neither optional nor negotiable, he said, adding that the Syrian regime was likely responsible for the recent attack on Douma. Regrettably, all attempts to fight impunity at the Council had failed. As evidenced by the Russian veto that once again had blocked action in the Council, some states were more interested in abusing the means of settling conflicts.

VI.3. The Rejection of the Russian Draft Resolution on 14 April 2018

50. In the meeting of the Security Council on 14 April 2018, the Secretary-General sent a clear message to its members in relation to the strikes in Syria.[55] It was his duty, he said, to remind the member states that there is an obligation to act consistently with the Charter and with international

55 United Nations, Secretary-General, Secretary-General's briefing to the Security Council on Syria, 14.4.2018.

law in general, and to urge them all to show restraint in those dangerous circumstances and to avoid acts that could escalate matters and worsen the suffering of the Syrian people. He continued by repeating – given that any use of chemical weapons is abhorrent – his deep disappointment that the Security Council failed to agree upon a dedicated mechanism for effective accountability, because a lack of accountability emboldens those who would use such weapons by providing them with the reassurance of impunity. And this in turn further weakens the norm proscribing the use of chemical weapons. The seriousness of the recent allegations of the use of chemical weapons in Douma required in any case a thorough investigation using impartial, independent and professional expertise. The OPCW Fact-Finding Mission was already in Syria and was ready to go to the site concerned. He was confident that they would have full access without any restrictions or impediments to perform their activities.

51. The Russian Federation submitted a draft resolution saying, inter alia, that the Security Council condemned the aggression against Syria by the United States and its allies in violation of international law and the UN Charter, and that this aggression against the sovereign territory of Syria took place at the moment the Fact-Finding Mission had just begun its work to collect evidence of the alleged use of chemical weapons in Douma.[56] It added that it had called for the meeting to discuss aggressive actions by the United States. It was shameful, its representative said, that, in justifying its aggression, that government had cited its Constitution. Washington, DC, must learn: the international code of behaviour regarding the use of force was regulated by the Charter. Its draft resolution, however, was defeated by a recorded vote of 8 against (including the United States, the United Kingdom, France and the Netherlands), 3 in favour (Bolivia, China and Russian Federation) and 4 abstentions (including Ethiopia and Peru).

52. The United States delegate replied, meanwhile, that the time for talk had ended the previous night when her country, along with the United Kingdom and France, had acted, not in revenge, punishment or a symbolic show of force, but to deter the future use of chemical weapons by holding the Syrian regime accountable. The targets selected were at the heart of the regime's illegal chemical weapons program, and the action taken by the three countries had been legitimate and proportional. Along those lines the delegate of the United Kingdom said that any state was permitted under international law to take measures to alleviate extreme humanitarian suffering. Nor was it illegal to use force to stop the use of chemical weapons. The representative of France said that his government had no doubt about the Assad regime's responsibility for the attack. By

56 Security Council, Draft Resolution, S/2018/355, 14.4.2018.

ordering the 7 April attack, the regime understood that it was testing the global threshold for tolerance. "Silence is no longer a solution," he stated, and the Council could no longer tolerate the trivialization of chemical weapons use.[57]

53. The representative of the Netherlands, Lise Gregoire-van Haaren, stated:

> "that the Syrian regime has left the world no doubt as to its willingness to unleash terror on its own population. The repeated use of chemical weapons counts as the most cynical expression of that campaign. Just a week ago, the world was yet again confronted with reports of chemical-weapons use – that time in Douma. All the while, the Russian Federation has made clear to the world its readiness to stand by Al-Assad every step of the way. It has blocked draft resolutions in the Council that could have stopped the violence. I call upon all members of the Security Council to support a collective, meaningful response to the use of chemical weapons. But even if the Council fails to act, it should be clear to the world that the use of chemical weapons is never permissible. Against the background of past horrors and the unabated risk of recurrence, the response by France, the United Kingdom and the United States is *understandable* [emphasis added]. The response was measured in targeting a limited number of military facilities that were used by the Syrian regime in the context of its illegal chemical-weapons arsenal. The action taken by those three countries made clear that the use of chemical weapons is unacceptable. Last night's response was aimed at reducing the capabilities to execute future chemical attacks. [...] The use of chemical weapons is a serious violation of international law and may constitute a war crime or crime against humanity. The Kingdom of the Netherlands strongly believes that the international community must fully uphold the standard that the use of chemical weapons is never permissible. Impunity cannot, and will not, prevail."[58]

A month later, on 17 May 2018, during a meeting of the Security Council concerning several issues (the rectification of the failure to prohibit the use of force and the maintenance of international peace), the Dutch Minister of Foreign Affairs, Stef Blok, said that even though Syria had seen a rampant trampling of international norms, the Council had witnessed the use of veto power a dozen times in seven years thwarting decisive action on a seven-year-old conflict that had ravaged the country and destabilized

57 The references to the statements of the United States, the United Kingdom and France are based upon the meetings coverage of the Security Council: Following air strikes against suspected chemical weapons sites in Syria: Security Council rejects proposal to condemn aggression, SC/13296, 14.4.2018.

58 Security Council, 8233rd meeting, S/PV.8233, 14.4.2018, p. 13.

the region. "The Council will force itself into irrelevance," he said. "The laws will again cede to arms. And we will all lose. If and when the Council makes itself irrelevant by inaction, other avenues will have to be explored" to ensure fundamental international norms were upheld. When a country was not able or willing to protect its citizens, the responsibility rested with the Council, meaning that those with veto power must use that privilege with maximum restraint. He wondered what would happen if it could be used as a licence to kill or a means to obstruct justice.[59]

VI.4. The Report of the OPCW Fact-Finding Mission on the Incident in Douma

54. In the foregoing paragraphs, it has become more than clear how crucial independent, impartial and qualified investigations into the (alleged) use of chemical weapons are for a grounded and balanced political debate on Syria and, if necessary or desirable, appropriate policy measures against the Syrian regime. It goes without saying that the OPCW plays an important role in this context. The OPCW's Fact-Finding Mission was set up in 2014 "to establish facts surrounding allegations of the use of toxic chemicals, reportedly chlorine, for hostile purposes in the Syrian Arab Republic". Its findings became the basis for the work of the OPCW-UN Joint Investigative Mechanism (JIM), which was established as an independent body in August 2015 to identify the perpetrators of the chemical weapon attacks confirmed by the Fact-Finding Mission. The Joint Investigative Mechanism's mandate, however, expired in November 2017 as the consequence of a veto from Russia against its extension.[60]

55. On 1 March 2019, the Technical Secretariat of the OPCW distributed the *Report of the Fact-Finding Mission regarding the incident of alleged use of toxic chemicals as a weapon in Douma, Syrian Arab Republic, on 7 April 2018.*[61] This report shows that it was not easy to execute the investigation, for example the Fact-Finding Mission team could not enter Douma until almost a week after their arrival due to the high security risk to the team "which included the presence of unexploded ordinance, explosives and sleeper cells", and the team did not have direct access to examine dead bodies, as it could not enter Douma until two weeks after the incident, by

59 Security Council, Security Council must rectify failure to prohibit use of force, maintain international peace, speakers stress in day-long debate, SC/13344, 17.5.2018.

60 The website of the OPCW refers to a number of documents concerning the history of these and other bodies of this important organization (https://opwc.unmissions.org).

61 OPCW, Technical Secretariat, S/1731/2019, 1.3.2019. As regards the start of this investigation see the related press reports of the OPCW dated 10.4.2018 and 14.4.2018. See also Schneider and Lütkefeld, 2019.

which time the bodies had been buried. Nevertheless, thanks to a number of investigative activities (on-site visits, chemical detection, environmental sample collection, witness and casualty interviews, reports by medical staff, etc.) the Fact-Finding Mission in the end came to the following general conclusion:

> "Regarding the alleged use of toxic chemicals as a weapon on 7 April 2018 in Douma [...] the evaluation and analysis of all the information gathered by the Fact-Finding Mission [...] provide reasonable grounds that the use of a toxic chemical as a weapon took place. This toxic chemical contained reactive chlorine. The toxic chemical was likely molecular chlorine."

It goes without saying that the Russian Federation and the Syrian regime are unwilling to accept this conclusion. This explains in any case not only why in recent months Russia-friendly media channels and groupings have suddenly started to promote the distribution of a report that would contradict the findings of the OPCW report, but also why the Syrian regime refuses to issue a visa to the head of the OPCW Investigations and Identification Team that would try to attribute responsibility for the poison gas attack on Douma.[62]

VII. SOME COMMENTS FROM THE ACADEMIC COMMUNITY

56. Not many academics specifically published their opinion in relation to the 14 April 2018 military response to the poison gas attack on 7 April 2018. The relevant authors can be divided in two categories:

    - Those authors who straightforwardly state that this response was illegal and that its justification for the most part lacks – in any case from an international law perspective – clarity and coherence;

    - Those authors who use the response to seek alternatives with regard to international law as it stands now in order to break the deadlock: the referral of cases from the Security Council to the General Assembly or a change of international law concerning humanitarian intervention.

57. In relation to the first category of authors one may refer to Thomas Van Poecke (KU Leuven), Olivier Corten (Université Libre de Bruxelles) and

62 See, for example, Lucas, Regime tries to block further investigation of Douma chlorine attack, *Syria Daily*, 26.5.2019; A. Maté, Top scientist slams OPCW leadership for repressing dissenting report on Syria gas attack, *Grayzone*, 18.6.2019; X., Russia does not rule out need for new Douma incident investigation – envoy to OPCW, TASS, 12.7.2018, and W. Heck, Wie zat er achter de gifgasaanval, *NRC*, 19.7.2019.

Nabil Hajjami (CEDIN Paris Nanterre), and Aniel De Beer and Dire Tladi (University of Johannesburg and University of Pretoria respectively):

- Van Poecke:[63] there is no doubt that this retaliatory military action in an international law perspective constitutes an illegal act of aggression; moreover it embodies the risk of further escalation of the conflict in Syria; this act could stimulate a claim from Syria and Russia that it would be allowed to attack the United States, the United Kingdom and France;

- Corten and Hajjami:[64] the legal basis of the response is divergent and ambiguous: armed retaliation (the United States), implicit authorization by the Security Council (France), and humanitarian intervention (the United Kingdom); the absence of a clear legal justification is compensated by a mix of moral, political and legal considerations; this response discredits international law and the United Nations; in name of a just cause every state can stand up as a private law enforcer;

- De Beer and Tladi:[65] in answer to the question as to whether a state, or group of states, can intervene militarily in another state in order to protect the population of the latter state under international law *as it currently stands* or, put a different way, whether the doctrine of humanitarian intervention can justify these strikes, one has to come to the conclusion that a careful analysis of statements and votes by the members of the Security Council in 14 April 2018 illustrates that there is no consistent support for the use of force on the basis of humanitarian intervention; if anything, justification for the use of force for humanitarian purposes is *ad hoc* and the basis for justification inconsistent, and as such, however much one would wish it so from a humanitarian perspective, it has no effect on the current state of law.

58. With regard to the second category of authors one may refer to Rebecca Barber (Deakin University), Dapo Akande (Oxford University) and Michael Scharf (Case Western Reserve University):

    - Barber:[66] from an international legal perspective, one of the most alarming aspects of the allied missile strike in Syria was the near-complete absence (save for in the British Parliament) of any reference to international law and the seeming irrelevance of the strike's illegality in the generally affirming remarks that followed; this follows a trend

63 T. van Poecke, Het internationaal recht alweer geschonden, *De Standaard*, 16.4.2018.

64 O. Corten and N. Hajjami, Les frappes des Etats-Unis, du Royaume-Uni et de la France en Syrie: quelles justifications juridiques?, Bruxelles, cdi.ulb.ac.be., 20.4.2018.

65 De Beer and Tladi, 2019.

66 Barber, 2018.

seen since the Cold War and particularly since Kosovo, whereby it is increasingly accepted that military interventions may be legitimate without being lawful, and that perhaps we should just accept this as *Realpolitik* and not be overly concerned; while this view raises alarm bells for most international lawyers, it is not without support; it is even a trend that, as articulated by many states following the events in Syria, is "understandable" and perhaps inevitable in light of the resounding failure of the Security Council – in Syria and elsewhere – to fulfil its responsibilities in the realm of international peace and security; ways must be found for "concerned states" who wish to act collectively to protect civilians from atrocities to do so within the bounds of the law; the answer lies in the UN Charter: maintenance of international peace and security is a purpose not just of the Security Council but of the UN writ large: "if it is the view of the majority of the Security Council that action is required on Syria, and that the Security Council has failed, it is incumbent upon this majority to refer the situation to the General Assembly. It is then incumbent upon the General Assembly to act on their secondary responsibility";

- Akande:[67] the position taken by the government is significantly flawed – there is neither a general state practice of humanitarian intervention nor is any such practice accepted as law; neither the United States nor France has ever advanced such a view of the law nor have they sought to provide any legal justification for the recent strikes; on the contrary, a large number of states has rejected this legal position; moreover, there is little *opinion juris* on which a doctrine of humanitarian intervention might be based under customary international law; if that legal position would be accepted by states globally, it would allow for individual assessments of when force was necessary to achieve humanitarian ends; perhaps the Uniting for Peace Resolution could allow the General Assembly to take measures in response to breaches of international peace, where the Council is blocked through the threat or use of force;
- Scharf:[68] taking into account the unique aspects of the Syrian air strikes, including the context of a crisis of historic proportions, the underlying humanitarian need to stop the use of chemical weapons against a civilian population, the collectivity of the action taken, the limited targets and collateral damage, the explicit invocation of humanitarian intervention by the United Kingdom as the legal justification, the

67 D. Akande, The legality of the UK's air strikes on the Assad government in Syria (Attachment to the report of the House of Commons, Foreign Affairs Committee, *Global Britain: the Responsibility to Protect and Humanitarian Intervention*, London, 2018).

68 Scharf, 2019a and 2019b.

United States' apparent adoption of that justification, the support of many states from all parts of the globe, and the refusal of the Security Council to condemn the air strikes, one may argue that the 14 April air strikes constitute a transformative event that has changed international law concerning humanitarian intervention: a Grotian moment marking a rapid change in customary international law and in the interpretation of the UN Charter concerning the right to use force for humanitarian intervention in the absence of Security Council authorization.

VIII. CONCLUDING REMARKS

59. Against the background of the severe political consequences – the fall of two Cabinets – of the inquiries into the involvement of the Netherlands in the Srebrenica massacre in 1995 and the attack on Iraq in 2003, it is quite understandable that in recent times successive Dutch governments have come to the conclusion that only in case of an explicit mandate of the Security Council can the Netherlands give its "support" to interstate use of force by third states and under certain conditions can only express its "understanding" for such use of force.

a. The distinction between "support" and "understanding" as it has been formulated above is predominantly a procedural one: the presence or absence of a mandate by the Security Council. This does not detract from the fact that in the case of the attack on Syria on 14 April 2018 – apart from the Netherlands – quite a large number of states in one way or another gave their "support" to this attack or expressed their "understanding" for the initiative by the three allied powers and made no (procedural) distinction, or any distinction at all, between these two terms. If one would nevertheless like to make a more substantive distinction between these two expressions, one could perhaps state that "understanding" is a passive form of "support" whereas "support" as such equates to an active form of "understanding".

b. It is remarkable that the three countries involved in the attack on Syria on 14 April 2018 despite their close military cooperation justified this attack with arguments that in terms of its *objectives,* on the one hand differ quite a lot from each other, and on the other hand strongly resemble one another:

Differences:

- In the case of the United States "national security interests" (stopping the humanitarian catastrophe, deterrence with regard to the use of chemical weapons, and regional stability) constitute the overarching justification;

- In the case of the United Kingdom "humanitarian intervention" is the fundamental justification: averting a humanitarian catastrophe, no intervention in a civil war or regime change;
- In the case of France the attack is justified by the necessity to enforce international law and this in three ways: by giving effect to Resolution 2118, by the absolute obligation to stop the use of chemical weapons, and by the confirmation that France still is a political and military power that feels called on to enforce international law in an effective manner; with hindsight a fourth argument arises: many states and international organizations support the position of France and its allies and reject the position of Russia on the attack in question – how could such an attack be in contradiction with legality?

Similarities:

- One has to stop the repeated use of those abhorrent chemical weapons in Syria as well as to prevent the proliferation of chemical weapons in the world, in particular them falling into the hands of dictators and terrorists;
- The use of chemical weapons is a very serious violation of a fundamental international norm, enshrined in the Chemical Weapons Convention; that violation embodies the risk of normalization of their use and such a development should be prevented at all costs: the norm must be upheld;
- There is always a high price to pay for inaction in cases like this because it not only encourages further erosion of the norm but also makes it harder to find a political solution.

In addition one may observe that, apart from the differences and similarities in terms of the *objectives* of the attack, the justifications by the three countries have – in terms of the *conditions* in which an armed interstate response to an incident like that in Douma on 7 April 2018 is acceptable – a lot in common:

- There was a significant body of information/evidence that a poison gas attack again took place, in Douma;
- The attack on Syria was in terms of proportionality a balanced response: specific targets, limited in time and place;

– In terms of subsidiarity there was no practicable (political, diplomatic or military) alternative to this attack;

– The use of force always has to be a weapon of last resort and this weapon can only be deployed if it is absolutely necessary, i.e. in extreme cases.

c. A comparison between the statements by NATO and the statements by (representatives of) important institutions of the EU shows that the related differences between these statements, generally speaking, involve minor issues. The difference that is most striking, in particular with regard to the explanation of vote by the Netherlands in the NAC, is that between the statement of the Secretary-General of NATO and the statement of the High Representative of the EU: *full support* for the military action versus *supportive of all efforts* to prevent the use of chemical weapons. These differences in opinion, however, are insignificant alongside the differences between the statements, on the one hand by the Russian Federation (and its allies, which sometimes includes China), and on the other hand by the United States (and its supporters) in the Security Council. It goes without saying that this confrontation with regard to the Syrian regime is the manifestation of the global power struggle between the political, economic and military heavyweights in the multipolar world we live in. Already for many years this struggle has made it very difficult, not to say impossible, to agree upon a common ground for a political solution of the multidimensional crisis in Syria and, in the wake of this impasse, to develop – for all parties involved – an acceptable "legal" or "legitimate" way to prevent or to stop mass atrocities by the Assad regime in that country. As the difficulties in relation to the role of the OPCW in this context demonstrate, it has become increasingly difficult even to collect in an impartial, independent and qualified manner the information or evidence that could be a truthful starting point for a rational discussion on allegations concerning the use of chemical weapons and on the measures which could or should be taken to stop or to prevent their use: investigative mechanisms are being thwarted or their results are being questioned by dubious methods.

d. In conjunction with the foregoing point, one should not lose sight of the fact that – even if it would have been possible to collect information and evidence in an unhindered and qualified manner on the poison gas attack on Douma and in this way fully meet the first (empirical) criterion in the British political doctrine of humanitarian intervention – the United States and France did not invoke in an explicit manner (like the United Kingdom) this theory to justify their participation in the attack on Syria. These two allies, as we have seen, made use of very different arguments to justify their armed intervention in Syria: national security interests and effective enforcement of international law. This is also one of the reasons why one has to conclude that the Douma case neither proves that humanitarian intervention – or responsibility to protect – has become the foundation of interstate use of force, nor suggests that the acceptance of this doctrine perhaps has reached a tipping point in states' practice, as some academics argue.[69] This conclusion is further strengthened by the fact that other academics, on the basis of a detailed analysis of the debate in the Security Council, have established that there was no consistent support for interstate use of force on the basis of humanitarian intervention. And one must never forget in this context the experts in international law who straightforwardly defend the position that the armed response of the allied forces to the poison gas attack on Douma was illegal because this means that also in terms of legal doctrine the theory of humanitarian intervention has not yet been accepted.

e. Is this impasse in academia, concerning the justification of interstate use of force that does not take place in the framework of one of the accepted exceptions to the rule that no force may be used between states, the end of the story? Such a conclusion would also be premature. Perhaps one should try to develop a different perspective on what is going on at an academic level as well as at a political level. Monica Hakimi and Jacob Cogan state that the current international law perspective more or less misses the point in relation to interstate use of force, namely that in this field two different codes operate: a state code and an institutional code, and that these two codes in fact interact quite smoothly with each other, albeit in a rather complicated manner.[70] This is exactly what we see in the Douma case: on the basis of different justifications, the United States, the United Kingdom and France came to act outside of the established realm of the United Nations, but did not really call into question the legitimacy of that institution. And conversely, the Secretary-General of the United Nations (like the majority of the members of the Security Council) did not explicitly condemn the military response by those three states to the poison gas attack on Douma. Perhaps the challenge is – with a view to the prevention or containment of contemporary humanitarian catastrophes – to look for more formal ways in which those two codes can be reconciled, not only in academic theory but also in political

69 See also Ercan, 2019.
70 Hakimi and Cogan, 2016.

practice. If such ways could be developed, the distinction between "support" and "understanding" for interstate use of force would become meaningless.

REFERENCES

Adviesraad Internationale Vraagstukken/Advisory Council on International Affairs and Commissie van Advies inzake Volkenrechtelijke Vraagstukken/Advisory Committee on Issues of Public International Law (2000), *Humanitaire interventie/Humanitarian Intervention*, Den Haag/The Hague.

Adviesraad Internationale Vraagstukken/Advisory Council on International Affairs (2004), *Preëmptief optreden/Pre-emptive Action*, Den Haag/The Hague.

Adviesraad Internationale Vraagstukken/Advisory Council on International Affairs (2010), *Nederland en de "Responsibility to Protect": de verantwoordelijkheid om mensen te beschermen tegen massale wreedheden/The Netherlands and the "Responsibility to Protect": The Responsibility to Protect People from Mass Atrocities*, Den Haag/The Hague.

Alkopher, T. (2016), From Kosovo to Syria: the transformation of NATO Secretaries-General's discourse on humanitarian intervention, *European Security*, vol. 25, no. 1, 49–71.

Averre, D. and L. Davies (2015), Russia, humanitarian intervention and the Responsibility to Protect: the case of Syria, *International Affairs*, vol. 91, no. 4, 813–834.

Barber, R. (2018), Uniting for peace not aggression: responding to chemical weapons in Syria without breaking the law, *Journal of Conflict & Security Law*, vol. 24, no. 1, 71–110.

Benjamin, A. (2018), Syria: the unbearable lightness of intervention, *Wisconsin International Law Journal*, vol. 35, no. 3, 515–548.

De Beer, A. and D. Tladi (2019), The use of force against Syria in response to alleged use of chemical weapons by Syria: a return to humanitarian intervention?, *Zeitschrift für ausländisches öffentliches Recht und Völkerrecht*, vol. 79, no. 2, 205–237.

Dunkelberg, A., R. Ingber, P. Pilai and E. Pothelet (2018), Mapping states' reactions to the Syria strikes of April 2018, http://www.justsecurity.org/, 22 April 2018.

Edwards, B. and M. Cacciatori (2018), The politics of international chemical weapon justice: the case of Syria, 2011–2017, *Contemporary Security Policy*, vol. 39, no. 2, 280–297.

Erameh, N. (2017), Humanitarian intervention, Syria and the politics of human rights protection, *International Journal of Human Rights*, vol. 21, no. 5, 517–530.

Ercan, P. (2019), UN General Assembly dialogues on the Responsibility to Protect and the use of force for humanitarian purposes, *Global Responsibility to Protect*, vol. 11, no. 3, 313–332.

Ferdinand, P. (2013), *The Positions of Russia and China at the UN Security Council in the Light of Recent Crises*, Brussels, European Parliament.

Gaskarth, J. (2016), The fiasco of the 2013 Syria votes: decline and denial in British foreign policy, *Journal of European Public Policy*, vol. 23, no. 5, 718–734.

Gramyk, E. (2014), Increased Franco-British military cooperation: the impetus, its results, and the impact on international humanitarian intervention, *San Diego International Law Journal*, vol. 15, no. 2, 377–423.

Hakimi, M. and J. Cogan (2016), The two codes on the use of force, *European Journal of International Law*, vol. 27, no. 2, 257–291.

Henderson, C. (2015), The UK government's legal opinion on forcible measures in response to the use of chemical weapons by the Syrian government, *International and Comparative Law Quarterly*, vol. 64, no. 1, 179–196.

Henriksen, A. (2018), Trump's missile strike on Syria and the legality of using force to deter chemical warfare, *Journal of Conflict & Security Law*, vol. 23, no. 1, 33–48.

Kaarbo, J. and D. Kenealy (2016), No, Prime Minister: explaining the House of Commons' vote on intervention in Syria, *European Security*, vol. 25, no. 1, 28–48.

Kaarbo, J. and D. Kenealy (2017), Precedents, parliaments, and foreign policy: historical analogy in the House of Commons vote on Syria, *West European Politics*, vol. 40, no. 1, 62–79.

Lagerwall, A. (2018), Threats of and actual military strikes against Syria – 2013 and 2017, in: T. Ruys, O. Corten and A. Hofer (eds.), *The Use of Force in International Law: A Case-Based approach*, Oxford, Oxford University Press.

Melling, G. and A. Dennett (2018), The Security Council veto and Syria: responding to mass atrocities through the "Uniting for Peace" resolution, *Indian Journal of International Law*, vol. 57, no. 3–4, 285–307.

Nahlawi, Y. (2016), The Responsibility to Protect and Obama's red line on Syria, *Global Responsibility to Protect*, vol. 8, no. 1, 76–101.

Netherlands Institute for War Documentation (2002), *Srebrenica, a "Safe" Area – Reconstruction, Background, Consequences and Analyses of the Fall of a Safe Area*, Amsterdam.

Odeyemi, C. (2016), Re-emerging powers and the impasse in the UNSC over R2P intervention in Syria, *Strategic Analysis*, vol. 40, no. 2, 122–149.

Qureshi, W. (2018), International law and military intervention: U.S. action in Syria, *University of Hawai'i Law Review*, vol. 40, no. 2, 115–154.

Ralph, J., J. Holland and K. Zhekova (2017), Before the vote: UK foreign policy discourse on Syria 2011–2013, *Review of International Studies*, vol. 43, no. 5, 875–897.

Rapport Commissie van Onderzoek Besluitvorming Irak (2010), Amsterdam, Boom (Commissie-Davids) (with a summary in English).

Ryngaert, C. and N. Schrijver, Lessons learned from the Srebrenica massacre: from UN peacekeeping reform to legal responsibility, *Netherlands International Law Review*, vol. 62, no. 2, 219–227.

Savarian, A. (2016), Humanitarian intervention after Syria, *Legal Studies*, vol. 36, no. 1, 20–47.

Scharf, M. (2019a), Responding to chemical weapons use in Syria, *Case Western Reserve Journal of International Law*, vol. 51, no. 1 & 2, 189–200.

Scharf, M. (2019b), Striking a Grotian moment: how the Syria airstrikes changed international law relating to humanitarian intervention, *Chicago Journal of International Law*, vol. 19, no. 2, 586–614.

Schmitt, M. and C. Ford (2017), Assessing U.S. justifications for using force in response to Syria's chemical attacks: an international law perspective, *Journal of National Security Law and Policy*, vol. 9, no. 2, 283–303.

Schneider, T. and T. Lütkefend (2019), *Nowhere to Hide: the Logic of Chemical Weapons Use in Syria*, Berlin, Global Public Policy Institute.

Stahn, C. (2013), Between law-breaking and law-making: Syria, humanitarian intervention and 'what the law ought to be', *Journal of Conflict & Security*, vol. 19, no. 1, 25–48.

Stravridis, S. (2016), The French parliament and the conflicts in Libya and Syria, *Mediterranean Quarterly*, vol. 27, no. 4, 21–41.

ANNEX E

Interstate Use of Force and Humanitarian Intervention: The Legal Framework and the Contemporary Academic Debate

Background Note by Joris Larik

 | DOI:10.1163/9789004445482_010

1. INTRODUCTION

1. As a complement to the background note on the positions concerning the 14 April 2018 military response to the poison gas attack on Douma assumed by the Netherlands and key allies, the present note provides a general overview of the relevant legal norms and the academic debate surrounding the issues of interstate use of force and humanitarian intervention, including reform proposals for the way forward. It does not claim to provide an exhaustive treatment of the subjects covered and the available literature on them. Rather, its intention is to provide context, background, and stimulate debate among the members of the Expert Group.

2. The two defining elements for the scope of the present enquiry are "interstate" and "use of force". In order to delineate more clearly the focus of this note, it should be pointed out at the outset what is not included within its scope. This note does not concern the use of force between state and non-state actors. This would include situations such as airstrikes (including drone strikes) against terrorist groups in another country, for example. These are sometimes justified by arguing that the state from whose territory the non-state group operates is "unable or unwilling" to address this threat.[1] While these can be seen as acts violating another country's territorial integrity, they are not necessarily instances of interstate use of force. Moreover, this note is not about international acts that do not amount to the "use of force", such as economic or diplomatic sanctions, regardless of their legality.

3. Legal norms and other normative frameworks are abstract concepts that have to be applied to real-life situations. Hence, attempts made in this note to provide an overview of different categories and types of conflicts and their applicable rules should in no way suggest that there is no fluidity in practice. Conflicts and their legal classification can change over time. For example, the US-led invasion of Afghanistan started as an international armed conflict against both the government, which was led by the Taliban at the time, and a non-state actor (Al-Qaeda), but later turned into a non-international armed conflict in which the new Afghan government fought the Taliban with international support. A single conflict theatre can also experience various forms of the use of force. The conflicts in Syria and Iraq are a case in point, as they have seen various forms of interstate and non-interstate uses of force. Moreover, modern technologies can cast doubt on the applicability of existing legal frameworks. For instance, opinions diverge on whether cyberattacks should be classified as use of

---

1 See Deeks, A., (2012), "Unwilling or Unable": Toward a Normative Framework for Extra-Territorial Self-Defense, *Virginia Journal of International Law*, vol. 52, no. 3, 483–550.

force.[2] NATO's Tallinn Manual 2.0 on the International Law Applicable to Cyber Operations simply notes that a "cyber operation constitutes a use of force when its scale and effects are comparable to non-cyber operations rising to the level of a use of force".[3]

4. With these preliminary observations in mind, the note proceeds as follows. Section II provides an overview of the relevant legal frameworks, with an emphasis on international law. Section III summarizes the academic debate on the legality and legitimacy of humanitarian intervention, while Section IV discusses prominent reform proposals. Section V adds a concise outline of the wider context in which the present enquiry takes place, while Section VI sums up the contents of the note and submits a number of questions for discussion within the Expert Group.

II. THE RELEVANT LEGAL PROVISIONS AND PRINCIPLES

5. For the Netherlands, the use of force in international relations is governed by its domestic law (in particular its constitutional law), to a limited extent EU law, and public international law – three separate but interlinked legal orders. After a brief overview of the first two aspects, the focus is put on the last-mentioned, seeing that the Expert Group is mandated to consider the use of interstate force in situations without a basis in international law. In order to delve into that question, it is essential to ascertain which legal bases for the interstate use of force currently exist, and where they find their limits.

II.1. Dutch Constitutional Law

6. Regarding the national foreign relations law dimension, countries usually maintain a set of criteria and a procedure under which the use of force can be authorized.[4] While certain national constitutions contain an outright ban on war,[5] others are less categorical about the renunciation of war

2 Gray, C. (2018), *International Law and the Use of Force*, 4th edition, Oxford, Oxford University Press, 34–35.

3 Schmitt, M. (ed.) (2017), *Tallinn Manual 2.0 on the International Law Applicable to Cyber Operations*, Cambridge, Cambridge University Press, Rule 69.

4 See Ginsburg, T. (2014), Chaining the Dog of War: Comparative Data, *Chicago Journal of International Law*, vol. 15, no. 1, 138–161; and Bradley, C. (2019), U.S. War Powers and the Potential Benefits of Comparativism, in: C. Bradley (ed.), *The Oxford Handbook of Comparative Foreign Relations Law*, Oxford, Oxford University Press.

5 Cf., e.g., Constitution of Japan, Art. 9; Constitution of Italy, Art. 11. See further Larik, J. (2016), *Foreign Policy Objectives in European Constitutional Law*, Oxford, Oxford University Press, 94–96.

in their domestic law. Other pertinent questions include the degree of parliamentary oversight,[6] and the national interests which can form a basis for using force.[7]

7. In the case of the Netherlands, its constitution (*Grondwet* in Dutch) does not include an outright renunciation of war. It does contain, however, a commitment that the Dutch armed forces shall be used "for the defence and protection of the interests of the Kingdom, and in order to maintain and promote the international legal order".[8] With regard to the Dutch Parliament, the *Grondwet* states that the government "shall inform the States General in advance if the armed forces are to be deployed or made available to maintain or promote the international legal order",[9] unless "compelling reasons exist to prevent the provision of information in advance".[10]

8. In addition, there is a general commitment that the Dutch government "shall promote the development of the international legal order".[11] This constitutional objective contains a dual duty. On the one hand, the Dutch government is obliged to abide by international law as it currently stands. On the other hand, it should also promote its further "development" or "perfection".[12] There is a sense of tension between these two dimensions, as the need for change implies current shortcomings, which, on their part, could dent the (moral) respect that international law commands and the degree to which compliance with it should be regarded as imperative.

II.2. European Union Law

9. As an EU Member State, the Netherlands is also subject to the primacy of EU law over national law.[13] Since the Lisbon Treaty reform and the

6 See, e.g., the War Powers Resolution (50 U.S.C. 1541–1548) in the United States.

7 See, e.g., United States Department of Justice, Memorandum Opinion for the Attorney General, Authority to Use Military Force in Libya, 1 April 2011.

8 Constitution of the Netherlands, Art. 97, para. 1. English translation used: www.government.nl/binaries/government/documents/regulations/2012/10/18/the-constitution-of-the-kingdom-of-the-netherlands-2008/the-constitution-of-the-kingdom-of-the-netherlands-2008.pdf.

9 Constitution of the Netherlands, Art. 100, para. 1.

10 Constitution of the Netherlands, Art. 100, para. 2.

11 Constitution of the Netherlands, Art. 90, para. 1.

12 See Vlemminx, F. (2019), Commentaar op artikel 90 van de Grondwet, in: E.M.H. Hirsch Ballin and G. Leenknegt (eds.), *Artikelsgewijs commentaar op de Grondwet*, Web edition 2019; also van Genugten, W. (2014), Sleutelen aan "het volkenrechtelijk mandaat", *Nederlands Juristenblad*, vol. 89, no. 37, 2628–2632, 2632.

13 Declaration No. 17 concerning primacy attached to the Lisbon Treaty, which in turn refers back to pertinent case law of the Court of Justice of the EU.

absorption of the Western European Union (WEU), the EU has become a collective defence arrangement. Member States have "an obligation of aid and assistance by all the means in their power, in accordance with Article 51 of the United Nations Charter" towards each other in case of armed aggression.[14] Moreover, the different tasks for which the Union's Common Security and Defence Policy (CSDP) can be used include, among others, "humanitarian and rescue tasks, [...] conflict prevention and peace-keeping tasks, tasks of combat forces in crisis management, including peace-making".[15]

10. However, the EU does not have "war powers" of its own, nor do the EU Treaties mention the concept of humanitarian intervention. "National security", moreover, is qualified as "the sole responsibility of each Member State".[16] EU Member States retain control over the CSDP, as well as the Common Foreign and Security Policy (CFSP) as a whole, through the principle of unanimity. Hence, the EU cannot compel the Netherlands to politically support any interstate use of force, let alone to partake in it. EU common positions and statements on issues relating to interstate use of force reflect in principle a consensus of all the Member States.

11. Moreover, since the Lisbon reform the Treaty on European Union (TEU) contains a similar commitment to that of Article 90 of the *Grondwet*. According to Article 3, paragraph 5 of the TEU, the EU is to contribute "to the strict observance and the development of international law, including respect for the principles of the United Nations Charter". Here, the two dimensions of compliance and further development are explicitly distinguished. It should be stressed that in the case of both the *Grondwet* and the TEU, these commitments do not only apply to a state's own behaviour. These formulations also include the promotion of respect for international law by others. Moreover, the TEU emphasizes the special importance of the UN Charter. However, it should be noted that it does not refer to the UN Charter as such, but rather to its "principles".

II.3. Public International Law

12. In tackling the question as to whether interstate use of force should be politically supported in cases where there is no basis in international law, an understanding of these bases and their respective scope is essential. These are mainly laid down in the provisions presented below. They can be subdivided into a general prohibition to use force, two exceptions

---

14 Treaty on European Union, Art. 42, para. 7 (TEU).
15 Art. 43, para. 1 TEU.
16 Art. 4, para. 2 TEU.

explicitly provided for in the UN Charter (self-defence and UN Security Council (UNSC) authorization), two largely accepted additional (quasi-) exceptions (rescuing nationals and intervention by invitation), and two generally unaccepted exceptions (armed reprisals and "Uniting for Peace"). Lastly, this sub-section highlights that certain kinds of interstate uses of force can incur individual criminal responsibility due to the activation of the jurisdiction of the International Criminal Court (ICC) over the crime of aggression.

II.3.a) The Prohibition to Use Force

13. The central norm in contemporary international law in this context is Article 2, paragraph 4 of the UN Charter, as one of the principles of the United Nations. It states that "[a]ll Members shall refrain in their international relations from the threat or use of force against the territorial integrity or political independence of any state, or in any other manner inconsistent with the Purposes of the United Nations." This provision is known as the "general prohibition" of the use of force in international relations. The prohibition to use force should also be seen in the light of the first line of the UN Charter's preamble, which stresses the determination of the international community "to save succeeding generations from the scourge of war, which twice in our lifetime has brought untold sorrow to mankind", referencing the two World Wars.

14. In addition, the prohibition to use force as enshrined in the UN Charter also exists as a norm of customary international law, to which scholarship generally accords the status of a peremptory norm of international law (*ius cogens*).[17] These norms are fundamental, overriding principles of international law. According to the Vienna Convention on the Law of Treaties a "treaty is void if, at the time of its conclusion, it conflicts with a peremptory norm of general international law".[18]

II.3.b) Exceptions Enshrined in the UN Charter: Self-defence and UN Security Council Authorization

15. The UN Charter provides for two exceptions to this general prohibition, i.e., self-defence and use of force authorized by the UN Security Council.

---

17 Orakhelashvili, A. (2015), Changing Jus Cogens through State Practice? The case of the prohibition to use force and its exceptions, in: M. Weller (ed.), *The Oxford Handbook of the Use of Force in International Law*, Oxford, Oxford University Press, 165.

18 Vienna Convention on the Law of Treaties, Art. 53.

16. Regarding self-defence, the UN Charter states that "nothing in the present Charter shall impair the inherent right of individual or collective self-defence if an armed attack occurs against a Member of the United Nations, until the Security Council has taken measures necessary to maintain international peace and security".[19] The threshold to be reached here is fairly high, i.e., an "armed attack" rather than other forms of lower intensity violence.[20] To be legal under international law, the use of force in self-defence is to be exercised in accordance with the principles of proportionality and necessity.[21]

17. To what extent the right to self-defence can be exercised before an armed attack has occurred, i.e. in a "pre-emptive" way, is a controversial issue. The general view among international lawyers seems to be that certain forms of self-defence in anticipation of an attack are permissible,[22] as long as a strict requirement of "imminence" of the attack is applied.[23]

18. Regarding use of force authorized by the UNSC, the Charter provides that the UNSC "may take such action by air, sea, or land forces as may be necessary to maintain or restore international peace and security".[24] However, this requires that the UNSC has determined "the existence of any threat to the peace, breach of the peace, or act of aggression"[25] and that non-forcible means, including economic sanctions "would be inadequate or have proved to be inadequate".[26]

19. According to the wording of the UN Charter, such resolutions "shall be made by an affirmative vote of nine members including the concurring votes of the permanent members".[27] In practice, however, this can come to be applied as nine votes without any explicit vote against ("veto") by any of the five permanent members.[28]

---

19 UN Charter, Art. 51.

20 Gray (2018), *International Law and the Use of Force*, 134–157.

21 See *Legality of the Threat or Use of Nuclear Weapons*, Advisory Opinion, ICJ Reports 1996, p. 226, para. 41.

22 Gray (2018), *International Law and the Use of Force*, 175.

23 Advisory Council on International Affairs (2004), Preëmptief optreden, Report No. 36, The Hague, July 2004, 34–35.

24 UN Charter, Art. 42.

25 UN Charter, Art. 39.

26 UN Charter, Art. 42; see also Art. 41 which lists the non-forcible means.

27 UN Charter, Art. 27, para. 3.

28 This has been confirmed by the International Court of Justice in *Legal Consequences for States of the Continued Presence of South Africa in Namibia (South West Africa) notwithstanding Security Council Resolution 276 (1970)*, Advisory Opinion, ICJ Reports 1971, p. 16, para. 22.

20. Such an authorization needs to be made explicit in the resolution. Scholars note that there is no such thing as an "implied" authorization by the Security Council.[29] Resolutions have to include the specific wording "all necessary means" to indicate that use of force has been allowed by the UNSC.

II.3.c) Other Generally Recognized (Quasi-)Exceptions: Rescuing Nationals and Intervention by Invitation

21. In addition to the two exceptions explicitly stated in the UN Charter, another two limited exceptions are largely accepted by the international community, i.e. the rescue of nationals abroad and intervention upon invitation (to use force) by another state. Rather than exceptions *stricto sensu*, they can rather be seen as falling outside the scope of the general prohibition to use force, since neither is strictly directed *against* another state.

22. This concerns, firstly, rescuing a country's own nationals by use of armed force. This exercise of using force has to be distinguished from humanitarian intervention and the Responsibility to Protect in that it does not concern protection of local populations. To date, the legality of such actions "remains largely undecided".[30] Moreover, one can distinguish between cases where nationals are rescued abroad from actors other than agents of the territorial state in limited operations (e.g. from terrorists/hijackers, as happened in the Israeli rescue operation in Entebbe in 1976), which are less controversial than cases where nationals are rescued from the authorities of the territorial state, which can be seen as an exercise of (low-intensity) interstate use of force.

23. Secondly, armed force on the territory of another state can be legally justified by an invitation from the latter state's government. Since this does not concern use of force against the armed forces of another state, this is technically not an instance of interstate use of force prohibited under Article 2, paragraph 4 of the UN Charter. Rather, it concerns instances where foreign help is requested to counter rebel groups or insurgents on an *ad hoc* basis. However, relying on such invitations can become

---

29 See Gray (2018), *International Law and the Use of Force*, 361–386 on attempts by states to argue for implied authorization.

30 Forteau, M. (2015), Rescuing Nationals Abroad, in M. Weller (ed.), *The Oxford Handbook of the Use of Force in International Law*, Oxford, Oxford University Press, 961.

controversial where the legitimacy of the government issuing it is unclear or in the case of a civil war.[31]

24. A novel variation on intervention by invitation is being developed on the African continent. Article 4(h) of the Constitutive Act of the African Union (AU) contains the "the right of the Union to intervene in a Member State pursuant to a decision of the Assembly in respect of grave circumstances, namely: war crimes, genocide and crimes against humanity".[32] From one point of view, this can be seen as a more general *ex ante* expression of consent to intervention in these scenarios.[33] However, from another point of view, this right to intervention stands in tension with a previous reference to the prohibition to the use of force between the AU's members and the general prohibition contained in the UN Charter, which overrides conflicting norms from other treaties.[34] The question as to whether UN Security Council authorization remains a requirement even for interventions under Article 4(h) of the Constitutive Act still "cannot be answered with certainty".[35] According to Christine Gray, in "practice the AU has not proved enthusiastic about forcible intervention without Security Council authority".[36] At the time of writing, the AU has not yet triggered Article 4(h).

II.3.d) Generally Unaccepted Exceptions: Armed Reprisals and "Uniting for Peace"

25. "Armed reprisals" and the Uniting for Peace Resolution are sometimes mentioned as possible additional exceptions to the general prohibition to use force. This, however, is generally rejected by the international legal community.

31 See De Wet, E. (2015), The modern practice of intervention by invitation in Africa and its implications for the prohibition of the use of force, *European Journal of International Law*, vol. 26, no. 4, 979–998, at 981.

32 Constitutive Act of the African Union, Art. 4(h); see further Kioko, B. (2003), The right of intervention under the African Union's Constitutive Act: From non-interference to non-intervention, *International Review of the Red Cross*, vol. 85, no. 852, 807–825.

33 Heller, K. (2018), Why Art. 4(h) of the AU's Constitutive Act Does Not Support UHI, *OpinioJuris* (23 April 2018), opiniojuris.org/2018/04/23/why-art-4h-of-the-au-constitutive-act-does-not-support-unilateral-humanitarian-intervention/.

34 UN Charter, Art. 103: "In the event of a conflict between the obligations of the Members of the United Nations under the present Charter and their obligations under any other international agreement, their obligations under the present Charter shall prevail."

35 Kunschak, M. (2014), The role of the United Nations Security Council in the implementation of Article 4(h), in: D. Kuwali and F. Viljoen (eds.), *Africa and the Responsibility to Protect: Article 4(h) of the African Union Constitutive Act*, Abingdon, Routledge, 66.

36 Gray (2018), *International Law and the Use of Force*, 56.

26. Firstly, "armed reprisals" denotes the idea that one or several states can force the cessation of grave violations of international law, such as the use of chemical weapons, by another state. Armed reprisals are explicitly prohibited in the UN General Assembly's (UNGA) "Friendly Relations Declaration" of 1970,[37] which is deemed to generally reflect customary international law.

27. Secondly, there is the Uniting for Peace Resolution. Already in 1950, the debate arose on how to deal with a deadlocked Security Council, in particular at the time "the strategy of the Union of Soviet Socialist Republics (USSR) to block any determination by the Security Council on measures to be taken in order to protect the Republic of Korea against the aggression launched against it by military forces from North Korea".[38] In an attempt to bypass such a deadlock, the General Assembly adopted Resolution 377 (V). Its main idea is that while the UN Security Council may have the "primary responsibility for the maintenance of international peace and security",[39] the UN General Assembly has a "secondary responsibility"[40] in this area.

28. In Section A of the resolution, it is noted that

> "if the Security Council, because of lack of unanimity of the permanent members, fails to exercise its primary responsibility for the maintenance of international peace and security in any case where there appears to be a threat to the peace, breach of the peace, or act of aggression, the General Assembly shall consider the matter immediately with a view to making appropriate recommendations to Members for collective measures, including in the case of a breach of the peace or act of aggression the use of armed force when necessary, to maintain or restore international peace and security."[41]

According to the UN Charter, the General Assembly decides on "important questions [...] by a two-thirds majority of the members present and voting", which includes "recommendations with respect to the maintenance of international peace and security".[42] Since "recommendations" are mentioned as the only measures the UNGA can adopt here, the resolution

---

37 UN General Assembly Resolution 2625 (XXV), 24 October 1970, Principle 1, para. 6. See also Art. 50 of the ILC's 2001 Articles on State Responsibility.

38 Tomuschat, C. (2008), *Uniting for Peace, introductory note*, United Nations Audiovisual Library of International Law, legal.un.org/avl/ha/ufp/ufp.html.

39 UN Charter, Art. 24, para. 1.

40 Barber, R. (2019), Uniting for Peace Not Aggression: Responding to Chemical Weapons in Syria Without Breaking the Law, *Journal of Conflict & Security Law*, vol. 24, no. 1, 71–110, 102.

41 UN General Assembly Resolution 377 (V), 3 November 1950, para. 1.

42 UN Charter, Art. 18, para. 2.

does not go so far as to claim a concurrent right for the UNGA to authorize the use of force.

II.3.e) The Crime of Aggression and Individual Criminal Responsibility

29. In addition, mention should also be made of the crime of aggression, seeing in particular that the Netherlands is not only a Member of the UN, but also Party to the Rome Statute of the International Criminal Court. Originally, the ICC Statute did not include a definition of the crime of aggression, which was deferred to a later stage. In 2010, the Parties to the Rome Statute decided on a definition at the review conference in Kampala in 2010 to be included in the Statute.[43]

30. The newly inserted Article 8*bis* of the Rome Statute defines the crime of aggression as "the planning, preparation, initiation or execution, by a person in a position effectively to exercise control over or to direct the political or military action of a State, of an act of aggression which, by its character, gravity and scale, constitutes a manifest violation of the Charter of the United Nations".[44]

31. In 2017, the Parties to the Rome Statute adopted a resolution that the amendment would not apply to states that have not ratified it.[45] The ICC's jurisdiction over the crime of aggression became effective on 17 July 2018. The Netherlands ratified the amendment in September 2016. Hence, the ICC's jurisdiction applies to the Netherlands with regard to the crime of aggression.

32. Some commentators have cautioned that the crime of aggression could have a "chilling effect" on *bona fide* humanitarian interventions.[46] However, the crime of aggression as defined in the Rome Statute operates with a high threshold, i.e., an act which "by its character, gravity and scale, constitutes a manifest violation of the Charter of the United Nations". These qualifications have led some authors to conclude that humanitarian intervention (assuming it is genuine, proportional, etc.) could not be considered a crime of aggression.[47] Nevertheless, it should be noted that

---

43 Rome Statute Review Conference, Resolution RC/Res.6, 11 June 2010.

44 ICC Statute, Art. 8*bis*, para. 1.

45 Assembly of State Parties to the Rome Statute, Resolution ICC-ASP/16/Res. 5, 14 December 2017.

46 See Ruys, T. (2018), Criminalizing aggression: how the future of the law on the use of force rests in the hands of the ICC, *European Journal of International Law*, vol. 29, no. 3, 887–917, 889 (footnote 8).

47 Kreß, C. (2017), Wird die humanitäre intervention strafbar?, *Frankfurter Allgemeine Zeitung*, 9 November 2017; also Ruys (2018), Criminalizing aggression, 891–897.

a United States proposal to that effect did not gain sufficient support at the Kampala conference.[48]

III. THE ACADEMIC DEBATE

33. The academic debate on the use of force and humanitarian intervention has been rich and fierce over the course of the past decades. At the present time, "there is a renewed debate about international law on the use of force".[49] It dwells on questions of both legality and morality, and the relationship between the two. Speaking in very broad terms, this debate can be subdivided into two opposing camps.[50] On the one hand, there are those who stress that interstate use of force, which does not fall within the recognized exceptions sketched out in the previous section, is illegal under international law, even if used for humanitarian purposes. They stress that there are also compelling moral reasons for maintaining a strict interpretation of the prohibition to use force. On the other hand, there are those who point out that regardless of the question of legality or illegality, there are certain moral imperatives to conduct such interventions, such as preventing mass atrocities. The following paragraphs will provide a brief overview of these different camps, including their respective appraisal of notable case studies and main legal and moral arguments as regards the current state of international law (*lex lata*). Section IV, in turn, will deal with specific proposals for changing the international legal framework (*de lege ferenda*).

III.1. Proponents of the Illegality of Humanitarian Intervention

34. For the proponents of the illegality of humanitarian intervention, legality and morality should not be approached as a binary choice. Legality per se can be seen as having moral significance. In "Just War Theory", the "right authority" is one of the classic criteria for determining whether going to war can be morally justified.[51] Following this logic, bypassing

---

48 Ruys (2018), Criminalizing aggression, 890.

49 Gray (2018), *International Law and the Use of Force*, 6.

50 Koh distinguishes three camps, the first of which consists of "those who always consider that practice illegal and illegitimate" and the second of "those who consider some forms of it 'illegal but legitimate'". His third camp consists of those "who believe we need a better law by which to evaluate its legality". The last-mentioned is dealt with here in section IV.1 below. Koh, H. (2017), Humanitarian Intervention: Time for Better Law, *American Journal of International Law Unbound*, vol. 111, 287–291, 291.

51 Pattison, J. (2012), *Humanitarian intervention and the responsibility to protect: who should intervene?*, Oxford, Oxford University Press, 43.

the legally enshrined authority of the UN Security Council detracts from moral desirability.

35. Moreover, many international law scholars stress that the general prohibition to use force is a major achievement in the development of international law and the pacification of international politics. International law should not enable war but be a "law against war".[52] According to Oliver Dörr, for instance, it represents "one of the cornerstones of the modern international legal order".[53] From this point of view, there is a moral imperative to prevent this prohibition from being watered down by expansive interpretations of existing exceptions or the proposition of new ones. Therefore, policymakers' choices in favour of (politically supporting) humanitarian intervention that is deemed illegal under current international law are to be condemned, despite any benefits of such interventions (e.g., saving lives, ending mass atrocities). Scholars from this camp tend to stress the risks of abuse of humanitarian interventions and advocate for restraint even in cases of mass suffering.

36. Similarly, some scholars stress that diluting the general prohibition to use force brings with it the risk of abuse, which could ultimately lead to eroding the post-World War II international legal order and security architecture. Indeed, "[o]ne of the most common arguments given in favour of the importance of an intervener's legal status amongst scholars, practitioners, and many states is that illegal humanitarian intervention involves abuse."[54]

37. Justifications based on moral grounds, moreover, can be counterproductive for developing international law further, according to Carsten Stahn. He notes that attempts to use moral arguments for enhancing political acceptance of interventions "is ultimately less supportive to formal 'normative change' than"[55] approaches that rely either on legal justifications or acknowledge illegality but plead in favour of excusing the offender. A "movement from legal patterns to arguments of political or moral desirability," he argues, "minimizes the 'precedential effect'" of particular cases.[56]

---

52 Corten, O. (2014), *Le droit contre la guerre*, 2nd edition, Paris, Pedone.

53 Dörr, O. (2015), Prohibition of use of force, *Max Planck Encyclopedia of Public International Law*, para. 1.

54 Pattison (2012), *Humanitarian intervention and the responsibility to protect*, 57.

55 Stahn, C. (2014), Between Law-breaking and Law-making: Syria, Humanitarian Intervention and "What the Law Ought to Be", *Journal of Conflict & Security Law*, vol. 19, no. 1, 25–48, 44.

56 Ibid.

38. Looking at state practice, Vaughan Lowe and Antonios Tzanakopoulos observe that "States are not willing to discard the prohibition of the use of force and the collective machinery of the UN in favour of the right of unilateral humanitarian intervention." [57] According to Dörr, "the great majority of legal writers refuse to accept the humanitarian purpose as sufficient ground for another exception to the basic rule against armed force".[58] He rejects the argument that humanitarian intervention would justify such an additional exception, "since the function of the prohibition of the use of force is not only to establish a core value of the international community, but also, and probably foremost, to deprive individual States of armed force as an instrument of their foreign policy".[59]

39. With regard to particular instances of interstate use of force for humanitarian purposes without a basis in international law, scholars that can be grouped within this camp condemn such acts and the attempts to justify them. For instance, "the majority of commentators agree" that the 1999 Kosovo intervention by NATO was unlawful.[60] Moreover, some scholars also consider the intervention "a 'dangerous precedent'".[61] The 2003 intervention in Iraq, in particular, is widely deemed "as a very serious violation of international law",[62] which could undermine "the credibility of collective security and of international law".[63] In addition, it has eroded trust among Western allies that initially supported the United States and gave credence to its allegations that Saddam Hussein's regime was developing weapons of mass destruction (WMDs). As argued by Willem van Genugten, for instance, it has made countries like the Netherlands more reluctant to openly support interventions that have no solid justification in international law.[64] This camp also includes those who criticize the NATO-led intervention in Libya of 2011 for having actively contributed to regime

57 Lowe, V. and Tzanakopoulos, A. (2011), Humanitarian intervention, *Max Planck Encyclopedia of Public International Law*, para. 47.

58 Dörr (2015), Prohibition of use of force, para. 46.

59 Dörr (2015), Prohibition of use of force, para. 46.

60 Franchini, D. and Tzanakopoulos, A. (2018), The Kosovo Crisis—1999, in: T. Ruys, O. Corten and A. Hofer (eds.), *The Use of Force in International Law: A Case-based Approach*, Oxford, Oxford University Press, 608.

61 Franchini and Tzanakopoulos (2018), The Kosovo Crisis, 619 (footnote 231 with further references).

62 Weller, M. (2018), The Iraq War—2003, in: T. Ruys, O. Corten and A. Hofer (eds.), *The Use of Force in International Law: A Case-based Approach*, Oxford, Oxford University Press, 659.

63 Ibid., 660.

64 van Genugten (2014), Sleutelen aan "het volkenrechtelijk mandaat", 2632.

change and therefore having exceeded the scope of the authorization to use force given by the UN Security Council in Resolution 1973 (2011).[65]

40. Responding to criticisms aimed at the veto powers of the permanent members of the UN Security Council and the related argument that humanitarian intervention is needed to bypass a gridlocked Security Council (see also below IV.3.), Irene Etzersdorfer and Ralph Janik note that the veto was an important reason for the United States and the (then) Soviet Union to join the UN in the first place.[66] This brings the discussion back full circle by emphasizing that the legal prohibition to use force is the bedrock of the current international system and that, while it is imperfect, we should be extremely cautious to erode it in any way.

III.2. Proponents of the Legitimacy of Humanitarian Intervention

41. The second camp contends in essence that while interstate use of force without justification under current international law is (technically) illegal, it can be morally justified nonetheless under certain circumstances, in particular for a humanitarian causes. This position often implies the (formal) illegality of the intervention but rejects this as the decisive factor for determining its moral desirability. Hence, policymakers' choices in favour of humanitarian intervention (and arguably for politically supporting it) tend to be lauded if they comply with certain criteria, even if the intervention is considered illegal from the point of view of existing international law. By contrast, policymakers' choices not to intervene are criticized as immoral, even if this would be law-abiding behaviour. Scholars from this camp highlight the costs of inaction, in particular the human suffering that could be prevented through humanitarian intervention, as well as the inadequacy of the current legal framework.

42. This academic camp consists chiefly of certain international lawyers and the epistemic community of "Just War Theory" scholars. For instance, they argue that an ethical discourse on legitimacy, drawing on the "Just War" tradition, can counter the narrowness of a legalistic debate.[67]

---

65 Posner, E. (2011), Outside the Law, *Foreign Policy* (25 October 2011), foreignpolicy.com/2011/10/25/outside-the-law/; see further on this debate Deeks, A. (2018), The NATO Intervention in Libya—2011, in: T. Ruys, O. Corten and A. Hofer (eds.), *The Use of Force in International Law: A Case-based Approach*, Oxford, Oxford University Press) 755–757.

66 Etzersdofer, I., and Janik, R. (2016), *Staat, Krieg und Schutzverantwortung*, Vienna, Facultas, 198.

67 Rudolf, P. (2017), *Zur Legitimität militärischer Gewalt*, Bonn, Bundeszentrale für politische Bildung, 128.

43. However, "Just War Theory" is no monolithic doctrine but includes vivid debates about the criteria for morally justifying the use of force. For instance, according to James Pattison, "an intervener's legal status according to current international law plays *little to no role* in its legitimacy".[68] Moreover, he argues that in terms of legitimacy "a pure and predominant humanitarian motive" is not necessary. An intervener can by all means be self-interested.[69] Similarly, he argues that, "whether an intervener's action results in a humanitarian outcome is irrelevant" regarding its legitimacy, as is the selectivity in conducting such interventions.[70] Instead, Pattison posits that "an intervener's effectiveness is the primary determinant of its legitimacy".[71] Similarly, Eamon Aloyo argues against the use of force having to be a measure of "last resort", as adhering to this principle can cause severe human suffering compared to intervening at an earlier stage.[72]

44. Scholars from this camp tend to criticize the current state of international law as increasingly inept for dealing with contemporary security challenges, in particular mass atrocities and large-scale human rights violations. In this context, it should be recalled that the UN Charter aims primarily at preventing *interstate* conflict, as a direct reaction to the World Wars which prompted its creation.[73] This current in the discourse notes a shift away from such conflicts towards non-international armed conflicts, such as civil wars and insurgencies, which then become the principal causes for mass atrocities and have destabilizing effects for wider regions and international security in general. The refugee flows from Syria and the use of chemical weapons are seen as stark examples of such spill-over effects. They criticize the international legal framework for only keeping pace with these shifts to a certain extent, such as the human rights revolution, but lagging behind when it comes to using force against other states that commit mass atrocities or fail to prevent them on their territory. Scholars from this camp point in particular to the massive human suffering and numbers of fatalities in cases where the international community failed to act or helped too little or too late. Egregious examples include the genocides in Rwanda and Srebrenica,[74] among other cases of mass atrocities such as in Darfur and Syria.

68 Pattison (2012), *Humanitarian intervention and the responsibility to protect*, 44 (emphasis in the original).

69 Ibid., 176.

70 Ibid., 176.

71 Ibid., 70. He calls this the "Moderate Instrumentalist Approach".

72 Aloyo, E. (2015), Just War Theory and the Last of Last Resort, *Ethics & International Affairs*, vol. 29, no. 2, 187–201.

73 Gray (2018), *International Law and the Use of Force*, 10.

74 See, e.g. Power, S. (2002), *A Problem from Hell: America and the Age of Genocide*, New York, Basic Books.

45. Instances where interventions took place without a basis in international law are lauded by these scholars, to the extent that they fulfil the various criteria posited for their moral assessment. For example, scholars from this camp would support the assertion that NATO's intervention in Kosovo in 1999 was "illegal but legitimate" because "all diplomatic avenues had been exhausted and because the intervention had the effect of liberating the majority population of Kosovo from a long period of oppression under Serbian rule".[75] Similarly, the 2011 intervention in Libya would be presented in a favourable light, at least at its outset. For Thomas Weiss, that intervention, since it was predominantly focussed on protecting civilians (at the start, before being aimed at regime change) was a turning point: "between 1999 and 2011 we witnessed not too much military intervention to protect human beings but rather not nearly enough".[76]

46. Regarding the argument that humanitarian intervention would set a "bad precedent"[77] and open the doors to abuse, Pattison offers a counterargument. He contends that "the worry that illegal humanitarian intervention will lead to abusive non-humanitarian intervention is largely misplaced",[78] certainly if compared to the abusive potential of other justificatory devices such as anticipatory/preventive self-defence for other reasons.

IV. ALTERNATIVES AND REFORM PROPOSALS

47. Beyond the current international legal framework regarding interstate use of force and humanitarian intervention, some scholars stress the need for reforms moving forward. Different proposals have been made, of which three prominent ones are outlined in this section. These are the "Responsibility to Protect" (often styled as "R2P"), the development of a new legal exception for humanitarian intervention, and ways to avoid UN Security Council deadlock in the face of mass atrocities.

48. In the discussion of reform proposals, it is important to bear in mind both the political and legal requirements to bring about change. For instance, if

75 Independent International Commission on Kosovo (2000), The Kosovo Report: Conflict, International Response, Lessons Learned, Oxford, Oxford University Press, 4. See also Koskenniemi, M. (2002), "The Lady Doth Protest Too Much": Kosovo, and the Turn to Ethics in International Law, *Modern law* Review, vol. 65, no. 2, 159–175, 162: "But most lawyers – including myself – have taken the ambivalent position that it was both formally illegal and morally necessary." See further references in Franchini and Tzanakopoulos (2018), The Kosovo Crisis—1999, 608 (footnote 137).

76 Weiss, T. (2011), R2P Alive and Well After Libya, *Ethics and International Affairs*, vol. 25, no. 3, 287–292, 291.

77 Pattison (2012), *Humanitarian intervention and the responsibility to protect*, 59–62.

78 Ibid., 62.

a reform proposal requires amendment of the UN Charter, the agreement of two-thirds of the General Assembly and the five permanent members of the Security Council is necessary.[79] For the development of a new norm of customary international law, both widespread state practice and a sense of legal obligation for that practice (*opinio iuris*) are required.[80] According to the International Court of Justice (ICJ), state practice should be "both extensive and virtually uniform".[81] However, as pointed out by Tullio Treves, this does not mean that this practice must "necessarily include all States nor must it be completely uniform".[82]

49. For changing a rule of *ius cogens*, which the prohibition to use of force is widely considered to be, particularly strong indications of a change may be required.[83] However, if the evidence in state practice required for such a change involves clear violations of current international law, this puts states into a difficult situation. Nevertheless, at least according to Michael Scharf, the 2018 airstrikes against Syria can be seen as the starting point of a crystallization of a new norm of customary international law, taking into account that "many states from all parts of the globe expressed support, while only a handful opposed the airstrikes".[84]

IV.1. The Responsibility to Protect (R2P)

50. As a way forward out of the conundrum of "illegal but legitimate" outlined above, the concept of the "Responsibility to Protect" was developed in 2001 in the Report of the International Commission on Intervention and State Sovereignty (ICISS).[85] It included three elements: the responsibility to prevent, to protect, and to rebuild. The second element in particular has sparked a vast amount of policy and academic commentary ever since.

51. As intimated in the ICISS report, the absence of authorization by the UN Security Council could be overcome with certain alternative courses of

---

79 UN Charter, Art. 108.

80 *Legality of the Threat or Use of Nuclear Weapons*, Advisory Opinion, para. 64.

81 *North Sea Continental Shelf*, Judgment, ICJ Reports 1969, p. 3, para. 74.

82 Treves, T. (2006), Customary International Law, *Max Planck Encyclopedia of Public International Law*, para. 34.

83 See Orakhelashvili (2015), Changing Jus Cogens through State Practice?, 157.

84 Scharf, M. (2019), Striking a Grotian Movement: How the Syrian Airstrikes Changed International Law Relating to Humanitarian Intervention, *Chicago Journal of International Law*, vol. 19, no. 2, 586–614, 613.

85 International Commission on Intervention and State Sovereignty (2001), *The Responsibility to Protect*, Ottawa, International Development Research Center.

action.[86] Firstly, it refers back to the Uniting for Peace Resolution of the General Assembly (see above II.3.d)). However, it acknowledges that the UNGA lacks the power to authorize the use of force. Nonetheless, it notes that "a decision by the General Assembly in favour of action, if supported by an overwhelming majority of member states, would provide a high degree of legitimacy for an intervention which subsequently took place, and encourage the Security Council to rethink its position".[87] As a second option, it mentions collective intervention by a regional or sub-regional organization. However, also here the ICISS notes the constraints of existing international law, according to which "the letter of the [UN] Charter requires action by regional organizations always to be subject to prior authorization from the Security Council".[88] Nevertheless, it contends that there are "cases when approval has been sought *ex post facto*, or after the event (Liberia and Sierra Leone), and there may be certain leeway for future action in this regard".[89]

52. In 2005, the UN General Assembly officially acknowledged R2P in the *World Summit Outcome*. The document noted three "pillars" of the Responsibility to Protect: the state's primary responsibility, the international community's responsibility to assist, and finally the international community's responsibility for timely and decisive action.[90] On the last-mentioned point, the UN members declared, *inter alia*, that "we are prepared to take collective action, in a timely and decisive manner, through the Security Council, in accordance with the Charter, including Chapter VII [...], should peaceful means be inadequate and national authorities are manifestly failing to protect their populations from genocide, war crimes, ethnic cleansing and crimes against humanity".[91]

53. The Libya intervention of 2011, which led to criticism of Western countries for allegedly exceeding the mandate provided by the UN Security Council

---

86 Ibid., 53 (point 6.28): "We have made abundantly clear our view that the Security Council should be the first port of call on any matter relating to military intervention for human protection purposes. But the question remains whether it should be the last. In view of the Council's past inability or unwillingness to fulfill the role expected of it, if the Security Council expressly rejects a proposal for intervention where humanitarian or human rights issues are significantly at stake, or the Council fails to deal with such a proposal within a reasonable time, it is difficult to argue that alternative means of discharging the responsibility to protect can be entirely discounted."

87 Ibid., 53 (point 6.30).

88 Ibid., 54 (point 6.35).

89 Ibid. Pattison (2012), *Humanitarian intervention and the responsibility to protect*, 236–239, also specifically recommends strengthening regional organizations.

90 UN General Assembly Resolution 60/1 of 16 September 2005, 2005 World Summit Outcome, A/RES/60/1, paras. 138–139.

91 Ibid., para. 139.

(see above), spawned a Brazilian initiative called the "Responsibility while Protecting".[92] The initiative highlights the importance of a strict sequencing of the three pillars of R2P as outlined in the *World Summit Outcome* document.

54. In sum, while R2P as an idea has received widespread political support, the UNGA's endorsement also brought it in line with the existing international legal framework regarding the use of force. This means that, through the lens of the UNGA, R2P does not provide an emerging additional exception to the prohibition to use force as laid down on Article 2, paragraph 4 of the UN Charter, and hence no legal basis for humanitarian intervention that could bypass the requirement for Security Council authorization.

IV.2. Humanitarian Intervention as a Legal Exception to-be-Developed

55. The proponents of making unauthorized humanitarian intervention legal under international law can be subdivided into, firstly, those who argue that there are alternative views on its legality already besides the "legalistic"/"positivist" one (as was shown in the previous subsection, R2P has not taken the route of being carved out as an alternative view on the law). Secondly, there are those who made specific proposals for reforming the existing legal framework.

56. In terms of alternative readings, according to James Pattison, a so-called "naturalist reading of international law" argues in favour of the legality of humanitarian intervention, drawing on "a human rights based approach that sees individuals as the subjects of international law and the role of international law as the protection of human rights".[93] According to this view, unauthorized interventions such as NATO's intervention in Kosovo in 1999 and even the US-led Iraq War of 2003 can be legally justified through a posited norm of customary international law.[94] Pattison, however, doubts that there is sufficient *opinio juris* for this point to be sustained,[95] which is an assessment that seems to be generally shared among international law scholars. It can be added that consistent state practice would also

92 Kenkel, K. and Stefan, C. (2016), Brazil and the 'responsibility while protecting' initiative: norms and the timing of diplomatic support, *Global Governance*, vol. 22, no. 1, 41–78.

93 Pattison (2012), *Humanitarian intervention and the responsibility to protect*, 49, referring to Téson, F. (2005), *Humanitarian Intervention: An Inquiry into Law and Morality*, 3rd edition, New York, Transnational Publishers.

94 Pattison (2012), *Humanitarian intervention and the responsibility to protect*, 49.

95 Ibid.

have to be demonstrated in order to posit a new norm of customary international law.

57. Moreover, according to Monica Hakimi and Jacob Katz Cogan, there are two "codes" regarding the use of force in international law. On the one hand, there is the "institutional code", through which UN organs, as well as regional organizations and the International Law Commission (ILC) "consistently aim to restrict unilateral uses of force".[96] This would seem to coincide largely with what is also called the "positivist" or "legalist" view, or indeed what has been sketched out in section II above. On the other hand, they contend that there is also a "state code" which "relies on states' horizontal and unstructured decisions in the context of specific incidents" and which "tolerate[s] much more unilateral force than does the institutional code".[97]

58. According to Hakimi and Katz Cogan, the interaction of both codes explains the operation of the current use of force regime in international law. They understand unauthorized humanitarian intervention to be a case of "conflict" between the state and institutional codes, albeit a muted one. While "[t]he vast majority of states accepted the institutional code's absolute prohibition as the authoritative statement of law", states conducting interventions "did not challenge this prohibition, and most third states either verbally endorsed it or stayed silent about the interventions".[98] However, they predict that the assertions that humanitarian intervention can be legal under circumstances are becoming more prominent, and so "the inter-code dynamic on humanitarian intervention is turning confrontational".[99]

59. Turning to specific proposals for reform,[100] according to Harold Hongju Koh, "[i]f we as international lawyers believe that international law should serve human purposes—including the protection of human rights, not just the territorial sovereignty of states", then the rule that unauthorized humanitarian intervention is always illegal under international law "cannot survive as the legal rule [...] in the Twenty-First Century".[101]

---

96 Hakimi, M. and Katz Cogan, J. (2016), The Two Codes on the Use of Force, *European Journal of International Law*, vol. 27, no. 2, 257–291, 261.

97 Ibid., 261.

98 Ibid., 276.

99 Ibid., 278.

100 For a useful comparison of different decision-making criteria regarding humanitarian intervention, see Bellamy, A. and McLoughlin, S. (2018), *Rethinking Humanitarian Intervention*, London, Palgrave, 153.

101 Koh (2017), Humanitarian Intervention, 288.

60. Hence, Koh puts forward a test for evaluating the international legality of humanitarian intervention, which involves six non-cumulative criteria. In summary, these are: 1) the presence of "a humanitarian crisis [that] creates consequences significantly disruptive of the international order including proliferation of chemical weapons"; 2) the absence of a Security Council resolution "because of a persistent veto", while "the group of nations that had persistently sought Security Council action had exhausted all other remedies reasonably available under the circumstances"; 3) limited use of force "for genuinely humanitarian purposes that was necessary and proportionate" and that "would demonstrably improve the humanitarian situation, and would terminate as soon as the threat is abated"; 4) collective action "e.g., involving the General Assembly's Uniting for Peace Resolution or regional arrangements"; 5) prevention of "the use of a per se illegal means by the territorial state, e.g., deployment of banned chemical weapons"; and 6) where the use of such means pursues "a per se illegal end, e.g., genocide, war crimes, crimes against humanity, or an avertable humanitarian disaster, such as the widespread slaughter of innocent civilians".[102] Koh also stresses the importance of providing "persuasive factual evidence" to substantiate each of the factors.[103] However, whether states will ever follow such standards for genuine humanitarian intervention, especially if compliance with such a standard cannot be monitored, can be doubted.[104]

61. In this context, it is worthwhile recalling a joint advice prepared by the Dutch Advisory Council on International Affairs and the Advisory Committee on Issues of Public International Law from 2000, which considered that "there are sufficient reasons, pending the further development of a justification based on international law, to consider humanitarian intervention admissible in extreme cases and as an 'emergency exit'".[105] In order to determine whether a particular intervention would be "admissible" (*toelaatbaar* in the Dutch version), the report proposed an assessment framework that requires answers to four main questions:

    i. Which states should be allowed to engage in humanitarian intervention?

    ii. When should states be allowed to engage in humanitarian intervention?

---

102 Ibid., 289.

103 Ibid.

104 Trapp, K. (2017), Unauthorized Military Interventions for the Public Good: A response to Harold Koh, *American Journal of International Law Unbound*, vol. 111, 292–296.

105 Advisory Council on International Affairs (AIV) and Advisory Committee on Issues of Public International Law (CAVV) (2000), *Humanitarian intervention*, The Hague, AIV secretariat, 35.

iii. What conditions should states satisfy during humanitarian intervention?

iv. When and in what way should states end their humanitarian intervention?[106]

62. In essence, the joint advice proposed that (i) states with a good human rights record, which are geographically close, acting as a group under the auspices of an international (regional) organization, should intervene (ii) after all non-military means have been exhausted for addressing a situation (or risk) of serious and large scale fundamental human rights violations requiring urgent intervention, when the recognized government of the state where the violations are taking place (or risk taking place) is unable or unwilling to address the situation, and when the humanitarian emergency can only be tackled by military means. During the intervention, (iii) the intervening states should act proportionately, respect international humanitarian law, avoid creating greater harm, limit their impact on the national structure of the country to a minimum, and report to the UN Security Council. In terms of ending the intervention, (iv) the intervening states should commit in advance to suspend the intervention as soon as the state concerned, the Security Council or a regional organization with UNSC authorization steps up to address the emergency, or in any event as soon as the intervening states' objective is reached.[107]

63. A set of criteria for humanitarian interventions has also been put forward by the United Kingdom government. It should be noted that the British government maintains the position that there already exists a legal right to such interventions if such conditions are fulfilled.[108] Though this position does not seem widely accepted, it could serve as a blueprint for an emerging future norm. The criteria proposed are:

i. there is convincing evidence, generally accepted by the international community as a whole, of extreme humanitarian distress on a large scale, requiring immediate and urgent relief;

ii. it must be objectively clear that there is no practicable alternative to the use of force if lives are to be saved; and

iii. the proposed use of force must be necessary and proportionate to the aim of relief of humanitarian suffering and must be strictly limited in

106 Ibid., 36

107 Ibid., 28–32 for the detailed explanations.

108 Prime Minister's Office, *Syria action – UK government legal position*, Policy paper, 14 April 2018.

time and in scope to this aim (i.e. the minimum necessary to achieve that end and for no other purpose).[109]

64. In view of such proposals, the question arises as to how they could possibly be implemented by changing the formal international legal norms in existence (the "institutional code" in Hakimi's and Katz Cogan's terminology). Here, we can distinguish three possibilities. Firstly, the UN Charter could be amended, though this requires the above-noted two-thirds majority in the General Assembly and the consent of the five permanent members of the Security Council, which in the case of Russia and China is unlikely to be forthcoming in the near future. Secondly, a new norm of customary international law could be developed. However, state practice, based on a sense of legal duty, would need to converge to the degree of being "virtually uniform". Even if that could be achieved, due to the UN Charter being an international treaty, which prevails over conflicting other treaties,[110] and due to the prohibition to use force being part of *ius cogens* (see above), it is highly questionable whether any new customary norm could trump the existing norms.[111] Thirdly, a new authoritative practice may emerge which "bends" the interpretation of the text of the UN Charter, as was the case with the exercise of voting rights of the permanent members of the Security Council, where the requirement of an "affirmative vote" was reinterpreted as the absence of a vote against (see above). However, this would also require general acquiescence, not least by the five permanent members whose prerogatives would likely be affected by such a reinterpretation.

IV.3. Avoiding UN Security Council Inaction

65. Rather than arguing for an additional exception to the general prohibition of the use of force in international law, another group of reform proposals aims at overcoming hurdles to obtaining UN Security Council authorization. These can be linked to the observation that the Security Council and its members are not above the law and "have to comply with any obligations that may arise from the UN Charter or from jus cogens".[112]

66. Here, two initiatives need to be distinguished: The Accountability, Coherence and Transparency (ACT) Group Code of Conduct and the French-Mexican initiative. The main difference between the two proposals

109 Ibid.

110 UN Charter, Art. 103.

111 Etzersdorfer and Janik (2016), *Staat, Krieg und Schutzverantwortung*, 194–195.

112 Kolb, A. (2018), *The UN Security Council Members' Responsibility to Protect*, Berlin, Springer, 525.

is that the former applies to all members of the Security Council, whereas the latter is addressed only to the five permanent members. In contrast to many other proposals for Security Council reform,[113] neither would require UN Charter amendment.

67. In 2015, the ACT Group proposed a "Code of conduct regarding Security Council action against genocide, crimes against humanity or war crimes" in a letter to the UN Secretary-General.[114] More than 110 countries support the initiative, including the United Kingdom, France, Germany, Belgium, and the Netherlands. The Code of Conduct contains a pledge to be made by all members of the UN Security Council, both permanent and elected, "to not vote against a credible draft resolution before the Security Council on timely and decisive action to end the commission of genocide, crimes against humanity or war crimes, or to prevent such crimes".[115]

68. Also in 2015, France and Mexico made a joint "Political statement on the suspension of the veto in case of mass atrocities" at the UN General Assembly.[116] In this statement, it is noted that "the Security Council should not be prevented by the use of veto from taking action with the aim of preventing or bringing an end to situations involving the commission of mass atrocities".[117] To this end, it proposes "a collective and voluntary agreement among the permanent members of the Security Council to the effect that the permanent members would refrain from using the veto in case of mass atrocities".[118] According to the French mission to the UN, "the initiative jointly led by France and Mexico is supported by 100 countries".[119] However, according to a news report from 2015, "[n]one of the other four veto powers – the United States, China, Britain and Russia – have formally signed up for the initiative".[120]

---

113 See, e.g., Nadin, P. (2016), *UN Security Council Reform*, Routledge, London.

114 UN General Assembly, Letter dated 14 December 2015 from the Permanent Representative of Liechtenstein to the United Nations addressed to the Secretary-General, A/70/621–S/2015/978, 14 December 2015.

115 Ibid., 3.

116 70th General Assembly of the United Nations, Political statement on the suspension of the veto in case of mass atrocities – Presented by France and Mexico, onu.delegfrance.org/IMG/pdf/2015_08_07_veto_political_declaration_en.pdf.

117 Ibid.

118 Ibid.

119 Permanent Mission of France to the United Nations in New York (2019), 5 things to know about France and the veto power, onu.delegfrance.org/5-things-to-know-about-France-and-the-veto-power (last updated 9 July 2019).

120 Charbonneau, L. and Irish, J. (2015), Dozens of nations back French appeal to limit use of U.N. veto, *Reuters* (1 October 2015), www.reuters.com/article/us-un-assembly-veto/dozens-of-nations-back-french-appeal-to-limit-use-of-u-n-veto-idUSKCN0RU30V20150930.

69. The French-Mexican proposal has its origins in an earlier French suggestion. In 2013, French Foreign Minister Laurent Fabius had proposed a code to restrict the use of the veto, though with the caveat that cases touching on "vital national interests" (*intérêts vitaux nationaux* in the original) of a permanent Security Council member would be excluded.[121] According to Noémie Blaise, the term "vital national interests" is too ill-defined and hence such an exception might defeat the purpose of effectively restricting the use of the veto.[122] Whether this caveat is supposed to be carried over into the French-Mexican initiative is unclear. It is not explicitly mentioned there.

70. The European Union and its Member States, in a statement to the UN General Assembly in June 2019, welcome both initiatives.[123] The United Kingdom government "whilst not officially endorsing the French proposal, has signed up" to the ACT Code of Conduct.[124]

v. THE WIDER CONTEXT

71. The debate on interstate use of force and humanitarian intervention takes place in the wider context of contemporary challenges to international security. The present section provides a brief overview of some of these challenges and how they relate to the present enquiry. These issues include the spread of armed violence, conflict prevention, a more competitive geopolitical environment and the protection of civilians during armed conflict.

v.1. The Spread of Armed Violence

72. Many regions of the world remain stricken by violent conflict, with certain trends towards deterioration. While interstate conflict has become relatively rare, internal conflicts are proliferating, with a count of more

---

121 Fabius, L. (2013), Réformer le droit de veto au Conseil de sécurité, *Le Monde*, 4 October 2013, www.lemonde.fr/idees/article/2013/10/04/reformer-le-droit-de-veto-au-conseil-de-securite-par-laurent-fabius_3489782_3232.html.

122 Blaise, N. (2017), *R2P et intervention humanitaire: Peut-on [ou comment] dépasser la volonté politique du Conseil de sécurité*, Limal, Anthemis, 251–252.

123 European External Action Service (2019), *EU Statement – United Nations General Assembly: Debate on the Responsibility to Protect and the Prevention of Genocide*, 27 June 2019, eeas.europa.eu/delegations/un-new-york/64721/eu-statement-%E2%80%93-united-nations-general-assembly-debate-responsibility-protect-and-prevention_en.

124 House of Commons Foreign Affairs Committee (2018), *Global Britain: The Responsibility to Protect and Humanitarian Intervention*, Twelfth Report of Session 2017–19, HC 1005 (10 September 2018) 12 (point 28).

than 400 in 2016.[125] According to the Global Peace Index 2019, the average level of "global peacefulness" has deteriorated since 2008, with the Middle East being "the key driver of the global deterioration in peacefulness".[126] Similarly, the Armed Conflict Location & Event Data Project (ACLED) noted that "the number of locations affected by disorder grew by nearly 15% across Africa, Asia and the Middle East in 2018, with an 11% increase in the geographic spread of organized political violence and a 24.5% increase for riots and protests".[127] This is the case despite "a slight overall decrease in the total number of political violence events in 2018, as well as the number of reported fatalities stemming from conflict".[128] Moreover, "[m]any conflicts now last a generation, or longer".[129]

73. Syria is highlighted in this context as one of the worst trouble spots. According to ACLED, "Syria is the deadliest place to be a civilian" seeing that "[n]early as many civilians were killed in Syria [in 2018] as in Nigeria, Yemen, Afghanistan, and the Philippines combined – the next four deadliest countries for civilians".[130] Nevertheless, according to the Global Peace Index, the defeat of ISIS/Daesh in Iraq and Syria "has led to an improvement in the security situation […] resulting in a decline in the level of violence and its economic impact".[131] As a result, "Afghanistan is now the least peaceful country in the world, replacing Syria, which is now the second least peaceful".[132]

74. This overall trend puts pressure on the international community to act, not least to contain spill overs from localized conflicts to wider regions. It increases calls for more humanitarian aid to be used in the service of conflict prevention.[133] In the most extreme cases, such conflicts will prompt calls for humanitarian intervention. As serious as the situation in Syria is, it is not the only place where mass atrocities are committed and are likely to be committed in the future. Answering the question of

---

125 Ministry of Europe and Foreign Affairs (*Ministère de l'Europe et des Affaires étrangères*), *Stratégie humanitaire de la République française 2018–2022*, Paris, 2018, 9.

126 Institute for Economics & Peace (2019), *Global Peace Index 2019: Measuring Peace in a Complex World*, Sydney, June 2019, 6.

127 Armed Conflict Location & Event Data Project (ACLED) (2019), *ACLED 2018: The Year in Review*, Madison, Wisconsin, ACLED, January 2019, 5.

128 Ibid., 7.

129 Department for International Development, *Saving lives, building resilience, reforming the system: the UK Government's Humanitarian Reform Policy*, London, 2017, 16.

130 Armed Conflict Location & Event Data Project (ACLED) (2019), *ACLED 2018*, 6.

131 Institute for Economics & Peace (2019), *Global Peace Index 2019*, 58.

132 Ibid., 2.

133 Ministry of Europe and Foreign Affairs (*Ministère de l'Europe et des Affaires étrangères*), Stratégie humanitaire, 9, noting that conflicts are at the origin of most humanitarian needs in the world.

whether humanitarian intervention should be carried out – or should be politically supported – needs to take into account a variety of possible future cases, which in certain respects will differ from the particular set of circumstances which prompted the airstrikes of April 2018 against the chemical weapons facilities in Syria.

V.2. Conflict Prevention

75. Successful conflict prevention makes humanitarian intervention unnecessary. For this reason, the original 2001 report introducing the Responsibility to Protect put the "responsibility to prevent" as the first element of the concept, before the responsibility to "protect", noting that "[p]revention is the single most important dimension of the responsibility to protect".[134] The third element, the "responsibility to rebuild", can also be seen as a form of preventive action in order to break the cycle of violence through peacebuilding.

76. During the past two decades, numerous armed conflicts have flared up, which can be seen as examples of failure to prevent conflicts. Pointing to successes of conflict prevention is a more difficult task, as it requires a counterfactual assessment of "what would have happened" in the absence of preventive action. The deployment of the United Nations Preventive Deployment Force (UNPREDEP) to Macedonia in 1992 is often credited as a success story in this regard.[135]

77. At the level of the United Nations, Edward Newman and Eamon Aloyo observe a "shift from a culture of reaction to a culture of prevention"[136] as well as a greater engagement of regional organizations in this area.[137] They distinguish conflict prevention that is "structural", i.e., aimed at the root causes of potential conflicts, and "proximate", i.e., concerned with the more immediate deterioration of a conflict.[138]

---

134 International Commission on Intervention and State Sovereignty (2001), *The Responsibility to Protect*, XI (Synopsis). The three elements from the 2001 ICISS report are not to be confused with its three "pillars" according to the UN General Assembly (see above).

135 Tardy, T. (2015), United Nations Preventive Deployment Force (UNPREDEP—Macedonia), in: J. Koops *et al.* (eds.), *The Oxford Handbook of United Nations Peacekeeping Operations*, Oxford, Oxford University Press, 500–510.

136 Newman, E. and Aloyo, E. (2018), Overcoming the Paradox of Conflict Prevention, in: W. Durch, J. Larik and R. Ponzio (eds.), *Just Security in an Undergoverned World*, Oxford, Oxford University Press, 50.

137 Ibid., 50–51.

138 Ibid., 52–54.

78. Regarding structural prevention, as noted by UN Secretary-General António Guterres, sustainable development is "one of the most effective tools we have to prevent conflict" as it helps "create resilient, stable societies and to address the root causes of violence of all kinds".[139] However, while structural prevention might decrease the number of potential cases requiring proximate intervention or even forcible humanitarian intervention, it is highly unlikely to eliminate them altogether in the foreseeable future.

v.3. Robust Peacekeeping and the Protection of Civilians

79. Seeing the spread of conflicts and failure to prevent them in many cases, another aspect which has received attention in the current discourse is that of enhancing the protection of civilians in armed conflict.

80. Concerning UN peacekeeping operations authorized by the Security Council, one of the recommendations from the 2000 Report of the Panel on United Nations Peace Operations (also known as the "Brahimi Report") was to provide peacekeepers with more robust mandates to protect not only themselves but also civilians against violence.[140] Nowadays, the Security Council has included the protection "'under imminent threat of physical violence' or a close variation thereof" in the mandates of several peacekeeping missions.[141] The mandates at times also make specific references to "the facilitation of the delivery of humanitarian assistance, and support to the return and resettlement of [internally displaced persons] and refugees".[142] In addition, "more recent operations have included specific language referencing vulnerable groups and the prevention of sexual and gender-based violence".[143]

81. Moreover, outside the context of UN peacekeeping operations, there have been calls for a greater focus on the protection of civilians during armed

---

139 United Nations Secretary-General (2019), Remarks at Security Council Meeting on Conflict Prevention and Mediation, 12 June 2019, www.un.org/sg/en/content/sg/speeches/2019-06-12/conflict-prevention-and-mediation-remarks-security-council.

140 United Nations, Report of the Panel on United Nations Peace Operations (2000), A/55/305–S/2000/809, Executive Summary, point 62; see also Holt V., Taylor, G., and Kelly, M. (2009), *Protecting Civilians in the Context of UN Peacekeeping Operations: Successes, Setbacks and Remaining Challenges*, New York, United Nations; and Hill, S. and Manea, A. (2018), Protection of Civilians: A NATO Perspective, *Utrecht Journal of International and European Law*, vol. 34, no. 2, 146–160.

141 Holt, Taylor and Kelly (2009), *Protecting Civilians in the Context of UN Peacekeeping Operations*, 43–44.

142 Ibid., 44.

143 Ibid.

conflict.[144] Despite this renewed focus, the Dutch Advisory Council on International Affairs concluded in 2016 that compliance with international law in this area is lacking and that "for many reasons, international military missions do not succeed in providing sufficient protection for the civilian population".[145] In fact, there is not even an officially agreed international definition for the "protection of civilians in armed conflict". As noted by the Advisory Council, Russia and China are wary of any definition of the concept that could be used to encroach upon national sovereignty and invite humanitarian interventions.[146]

v.4. A More Competitive Geopolitical Environment

82. Some if not all of the challenges sketched out above could be addressed if the most powerful countries in the world worked together. Instead, what is currently being observed is an increase in geopolitical tensions. According to the 2019 Munich Security Report, "the world is entering a new era of great power competition".[147] This seems also to be the threat perception in the United States, where the 2017 National Security Strategy noted "the growing political, economic, and military competitions" the United States faces in the world. In particular, it continued, "China and Russia challenge American power, influence, and interests, attempting to erode American security and prosperity".[148]

83. The pressure that such a more competitive environment puts on the global governance system was highlighted in a joint op-ed by the French and German Foreign Ministers from February 2019:

> "Unfortunately, it can no longer be taken for granted that an international rules-based system is seen by all as the best guarantor of our security and prosperity. [...] Some players are increasingly engaging in power politics, thus undermining the idea of a rules-based order with a view to enforcing the law of the strong. [...] The rivalry among

144 International Committee of the Red Cross (2012), *Enhancing Protection for Civilians in Armed Conflict and other Situations of Violence*, 2nd edition, Geneva, International Committee of the Red Cross.

145 Advisory Council on International Affairs (2016), The Protection of Civilians in Armed Conflict: Well-Trodden Paths and New ways Forward, Report No. 102, The Hague, July 2016, 7.

146 Ibid., 9.

147 Munich Security Conference (2019), *Munich Security Report 2019 The Great Puzzle: Who Will Pick Up the Pieces?*, Stiftung Münchner Sicherheitskonferenz, February 2019, 6.

148 The White House (2017), *National Security Strategy of the United States of America*, December 2017, 2.

major powers and growing nationalism have resulted in an increasingly fragmented world order – in political, economic and social terms."[149]

84. Great power disagreements, for instance expressed in the form of Russian and Chinese vetoes, go to the heart of the problem of a deadlocked UN Security Council. While certain forcible interventions in the 1990s where authorized by the Security Council, such as against Iraq in 1991 (Resolution 678(1990)) and in Haiti in 1994 (Resolution 940), Russia and at times China have vetoed such interventions in the more recent past. These situations should be distinguished from peacekeeping operations with a mandate to use force as these operations generally involve also the consent of the "host state" and other conflict parties.[150] According to Christine Gray, "[c]ertainly the inter-state use of force in the years since 1991 has not produced anything like the international response triggered by the Iraqi invasion of Kuwait".[151] Instead, "the reaction of the Security Council to the outbreak of inter-state conflict since the end of the Cold War, just as during the Cold War, has generally been to avoid condemnation and the attribution of responsibility and rather to call for a ceasefire and the restoration of peace".[152]

85. Therefore, it seems highly unlikely that permanent members of the Security Council will start supporting any humanitarian intervention in the near future if such an intervention could – from their respective points of view – adversely affect their national interests, including their relative geostrategic position. As a result, countries contemplating interstate use of force for humanitarian purposes will likely continue to face the choice between acting without a basis in international law or desisting from such actions for the foreseeable future.

86. In sum, the wider context surrounding the discussion about the interstate use of force and humanitarian intervention reveals several additional pressures on states when considering whether or not to take part in – or politically support – such operations. Violent conflicts are spreading and last longer. Conflict prevention tools are lacking in effectiveness. Even where interventions or robust peacekeeping operations take place with the express focus on protecting civilians, this has proven difficult in practice. Lastly, obtaining UN Security Council authorization, let alone

---

149 Le Drian, J.-Y. and Maas, H. (2019), Who, if not us? An alliance for multilateralism, originally published in the newspaper *Süddeutsche Zeitung*, English version reproduced in: onu.delegfrance.org/Who-if-not-us-An-alliance-for-multilateralism.

150 See Sebastián, S. and Gorur, A. (2018) U.N. Peacekeeping and Host-State Consent: How Missions Navigate Relationships with Governments, The Stimson Center, March 2018.

151 Gray (2018), *International Law and the Use of Force*, 328.

152 Ibid.

reforming the existing system, is unlikely due to a less cooperative and more competitive geopolitical environment.

VI. CONCLUDING REMARKS

87. The present note had three aims. Firstly, in the first two substantive sections, it provided an overview of the relevant existing legal principles and frameworks governing the interstate use of force and humanitarian intervention and of the academic debate surrounding this issue area. Certain grey zones and definitional issues notwithstanding, among legal scholars there is widespread agreement on the main principles and clarity, for the most part, under which circumstances recent examples of interstate use of force have been *legal* or not. An independent right to forceful humanitarian intervention without authorization by the Security Council is almost universally rejected, with the notable exception of the United Kingdom government's position. In sum, even though the existing rules can lead to morally undesirable constraints in certain instances, such as having to refrain from forcibly preventing or ending mass atrocities, they seem largely unambiguous in this regard.

88. Secondly, the note aimed to provide an overview of prominent reform ideas and situate the discussion in a wider context. What stands out here is: firstly, a general sense of frustration that the existing rules are being abused, e.g. by vetoes that block Security Council action to address mass atrocities; secondly, a fierce but unresolved debate on how to appraise interventions that have no basis in international law as it currently stands; thirdly, a widening gap and potential for open confrontation between state practice and legal (academic/institutional) discourse; and fourthly, a general sparsity of innovative reform proposals with the capacity to lead to real change. Arguably the most prominent recent push for innovation, the Responsibility to Protect, has been generally endorsed by the international community, but in doing so has been brought back in line with the existing rules. Moreover, even if there was widespread agreement on a new set of legal rules, the *how* question remains as the next daunting hurdle.

89. This gridlocked situation is exacerbated further by an unforgiving wider context, which is marked by a proliferation of conflicts, inadequate conflict prevention tools, the targeting of civilians, and more great power competition. Better conflict prevention and efforts to protect civilians in peacekeeping operations can alleviate the need for humanitarian interventions to some extent, but they will not remove it. Against this backdrop, it is likely that states will continue to face the difficult choice

between standing idly by in the face of mass atrocities or taking action in breach of international law.

90. Thirdly, the note closes by raising a number of questions to stimulate debate among the members of the Expert Group in view of what was presented here:

    i. To what extent are the arguments according to which considerations of legality in international law should prevail over questions of legitimacy still valid today?

    ii. Which set of criteria for justifying humanitarian interventions should be used in cases where they do not have a basis in international law? How can such criteria be monitored?

    iii. In particular, how can assessment criteria be formulated in such a way that they adequately address a situation such as the use of chemical weapons in Syria, but also other likely scenarios with different characteristics?

    iv. Should the illegality of humanitarian interventions be openly acknowledged by those who support them? Or should their legality be postulated with a view to developing a new norm of international law?

    v. How could a new set of criteria be turned into a new legal norm, taking into account the hurdles involved in developing international law on this issue? Which actors would need to be engaged? What is a realistic timeframe for effecting a change in international law?

REFERENCES

Adviesraad Internationale Vraagstukken en Commissie van advies inzake Volkenrechtelijke Vraagstukken /Advisory Council on International Affairs and Advisory Committee on Issues of Public International Law (2000), *Humanitaire interventie/Humanitarian Intervention*, The Hague, AIV secretariat.

Adviesraad Internationale Vraagstukken /Advisory Council on International Affairs (2004), *Preëmptief optreden/Pre-emptive Action*, The Hague, AIV secretariat.

Adviesraad Internationale Vraagstukken /Advisory Council on International Affairs (2016), *De bescherming van de burgerbevolking in gewapend conflict over gebaande paden en nieuwe wegen/The Protection of Civilians in Armed Conflict: Well-Trodden Paths and New Ways Forward*, The Hague, AIV secretariat.

Aloyo, E. (2015), Just war theory and the last of last resort, *Ethics & International Affairs*, vol. 29, no. 2, 187–201.

Barber, R. (2019), Uniting for peace not aggression: responding to chemical weapons in Syria without breaking the law, *Journal of Conflict & Security Law*, vol. 24, no. 1, 71–110.

Bellamy, A. and S. McLoughlin (2018), *Rethinking Humanitarian Intervention*, London, Palgrave.

Blaise, N. (2017), *R2P et intervention humanitaire: peut-on [ou comment] dépasser la volonté politique du Conseil de sécurité*, Limal, Anthemis.

Bradley, C. (2019), U.S. war powers and the potential benefits of comparativism, in: C. Bradley (ed.), *The Oxford Handbook of Comparative Foreign Relations Law*, Oxford, Oxford University Press, 753–770.

Charbonneau, L. and J. Irish (2015), Dozens of nations back French appeal to limit use of U.N. veto, *Reuters*, 1 October 2015, www.reuters.com/article/us-un-assembly-veto/dozens-of-nations-back-french-appeal-to-limit-use-of-u-n-veto-idUSKCN0RU30V20150930.

Corten, O. (2014), *Le droit contre la guerre*, 2nd edition, Paris, Pedone.

Department for International Development (2017), *Saving Lives, Building Resilience, Reforming the System: the UK Government's Humanitarian Reform Policy*, London.

De Wet, E. (2015), The modern practice of intervention by invitation in Africa and its implications for the prohibition of the use of force, *European Journal of International Law*, vol. 26, no. 4, 979–998.

Deeks, A., (2012), "Unwilling or Unable": toward a normative framework for extra-territorial self-defense, *Virginia Journal of International Law*, vol. 52, no. 3, 483–550.

Deeks, A. (2018), The NATO intervention in Libya—2011, in: T. Ruys, O. Corten and A. Hofer (eds.), *The Use of Force in International Law: A Case-Based Approach*, Oxford, Oxford University Press, 749–759.

Dörr, O. (2015), Prohibition of use of force, *Max Planck Encyclopedia of Public International Law.*

Etzersdofer, I. and R. Janik (2016), *Staat, Krieg und Schutzverantwortung*, Vienna, Facultas.

Fabius, L. (2013), Réformer le droit de veto au Conseil de sécurité, *Le Monde*, 4 October 2013, www.lemonde.fr/idees/article/2013/10/04/reformer-le-droit-de-veto-au-conseil-de-securite-par-laurent-fabius_3489782_3232.html.

Field, M. and M. Wright (2018), Russian trolls sent thousands of pro-Leave messages on day of Brexit referendum, Twitter data reveals, *The Telegraph*, 17 October 2018, www.telegraph.co.uk/technology/2018/10/17/russian-iranian-twitter-trolls-sent-10-million-tweets-fake-news/.

Forteau, M. (2015), Rescuing nationals abroad, in: M. Weller (ed.), *The Oxford Handbook of the Use of Force in International Law*, Oxford, Oxford University Press, 947–961.

Franchini, D. and A. Tzanakopoulos (2018), The Kosovo Crisis—1999, in: T. Ruys, O. Corten and A. Hofer (eds.), *The Use of Force in International Law: A Case-based Approach*, Oxford, Oxford University Press, 594–622.

Ginsburg, T. (2014), Chaining the dog of war: comparative data, *Chicago Journal of International Law*, vol. 15, no. 1, 138–161.

Gray, C. (2018), *International Law and the Use of Force*, 4th edition, Oxford, Oxford University Press.

Hakimi, M. and J. Cogan (2016), The two codes on the use of force, *European Journal of International Law*, vol. 27, no. 2, 257–291.

Heller, K. (2018), Why art. 4(h) of the AU's Constitutive Act does not support UHI, *OpinioJuris*, 23 April 2018, opiniojuris.org/2018/04/23/why-art-4h-of-the-au-constitutive-act-does-not-support-unilateral-humanitarian-intervention/.

Hill, S. and A. Manea (2018), Protection of civilians: a NATO perspective, *Utrecht Journal of International and European Law*, vol. 34, no. 2, 146–160.

Holt, V., G. Taylor and M. Kelly (2009), *Protecting Civilians in the Context of UN Peacekeeping Operations: Successes, Setbacks and Remaining Challenges*, New York, United Nations.

Independent International Commission on Kosovo (2000), *The Kosovo Report: Conflict, International Response, Lessons Learned*, Oxford, Oxford University Press.

Institute for Economics & Peace (2019), *Global Peace Index 2019: Measuring Peace in a Complex World*, Sydney.

International Commission on Intervention and State Sovereignty (2001), *The Responsibility to Protect*, Ottawa, International Development Research Center.

International Committee of the Red Cross (2012), *Enhancing Protection for Civilians in Armed Conflict and other Situations of Violence*, 2nd edition, Geneva, International Committee of the Red Cross.

Kenkel, K. and C. Stefan (2016), Brazil and the 'responsibility while protecting' initiative: norms and the timing of diplomatic support, *Global Governance*, vol. 22, no. 1, 41–78.

Kioko, B. (2003), The right of intervention under the African Union's Constitutive Act: from non-interference to non-intervention, *International Review of the Red Cross*, vol. 85, no. 852, 807–825.

Koh, H. (2017), Humanitarian intervention: time for better law, *American Journal of International Law Unbound*, vol. 111, 287–291.

Kolb, A. (2018), *The UN Security Council Members' Responsibility to Protect*, Berlin, Springer.

Koskenniemi, M. (2002), "The Lady Doth Protest Too Much": Kosovo, and the turn to ethics in international law, *Modern Law Review*, vol. 65, no. 2, 159–175.

Kreß, C. (2017), Wird die humanitäre Intervention strafbar?, *Frankfurter Allgemeine Zeitung*, 9 November 2017.

Kunschak, M. (2014), The role of the United Nations Security Council in the implementation of Article 4(h), in: D. Kuwali and F. Viljoen (eds.), *Africa and the Responsibility to Protect: Article 4(h) of the African Union Constitutive Act*, Abingdon, Routledge, 54–68.

Larik, J. (2016), *Foreign Policy Objectives in European Constitutional Law*, Oxford, Oxford University Press.

Le Drian, J. and H. Maas (2019), Who, if not us? An alliance for multilateralism, originally published in the newspaper *Süddeutsche Zeitung*, English version reproduced in: onu.delegfrance.org/Who-if-not-us-An-alliance-for-multilateralism.

Lowe, V. and A. Tzanakopoulos (2011), Humanitarian intervention, *Max Planck Encyclopedia of Public International Law.*

Ministère de l'Europe et des Affaires étrangères/Ministry of Europe and Foreign Affairs (2018), *Stratégie humanitaire de la République française 2018–2022*, Paris.

Munich Security Conference (2019), *Munich Security Report 2019 The Great Puzzle: Who Will Pick Up the Pieces?*, München, Stiftung Münchner Sicherheitskonferenz.

Nadin, P. (2016), *UN Security Council Reform*, London, Routledge.

Newman, E. and E. Aloyo (2018), Overcoming the paradox of conflict prevention, in: W. Durch, J. Larik and R. Ponzio (eds.), *Just Security in an Undergoverned World*, Oxford, Oxford University Press, 43–69.

Orakhelashvili, A. (2015), Changing *jus cogens* through state practice? The case of the prohibition to use force and its exceptions, in: M. Weller (ed.), *The Oxford Handbook of the Use of Force in International Law*, Oxford, Oxford University Press, 157–178.

Pattison, J. (2012), *Humanitarian Intervention and the Responsibility to Protect: Who Should Intervene?*, Oxford, Oxford University Press.

Posner, E. (2011), Outside the law, *Foreign Policy*, 25 October 2011, foreignpolicy.com/2011/10/25/outside-the-law/.

Power, S. (2002), *A Problem from Hell: America and the Age of Genocide*, New York, Basic Books.

Prime Minister's Office, *Syria Action – UK Government Legal Position*, Policy paper, 14 April 2018.

Rudolf, P. (2017), *Zur Legitimität militärischer Gewalt*, Bonn, Bundeszentrale für politische Bildung.

Ruys, T. (2018), Criminalizing aggression: how the future of the law on the use of force rests in the hands of the ICC, *European Journal of International Law*, vol. 29, no. 3, 887–917.

Scharf, M. (2019), Striking a Grotian Movement: how the Syrian airstrikes changed international law relating to humanitarian intervention, *Chicago Journal of International Law*, vol. 19, no. 2, 586–614.

Schmitt, M. (ed.) (2017), *Tallinn Manual 2.0 on the International Law Applicable to Cyber Operations*, Cambridge, Cambridge University Press.

Sebastián, S. and A. Gorur (2018) *U.N. Peacekeeping and Host-State Consent: How Missions Navigate Relationships with Governments*, Washington DC, The Stimson Center.

Stahn, C. (2014), Between law-breaking and law-making: Syria, humanitarian intervention and "What the Law Ought to Be", *Journal of Conflict & Security Law*, vol. 19, no. 1, 25–48.

Tardy, T. (2015), United Nations Preventive Deployment Force (UNPREDEP—Macedonia), in: J. Koops *et al.* (eds.), *The Oxford Handbook of United Nations Peacekeeping Operations*, Oxford, Oxford University Press, 500–510.

Téson, F. (2005), *Humanitarian Intervention: An Inquiry into Law and Morality*, New York, Transnational Publishers.

Tomuschat, C. (2008), *Uniting for peace, introductory note*, United Nations Audiovisual Library of International Law, legal.un.org/avl/ha/ufp/ufp.html.

Trapp, K. (2017), Unauthorized military interventions for the public good: a response to Harold Koh, *American Journal of International Law Unbound*, vol. 111, 292–296.

Treves, T. (2006), Customary international law, *Max Planck Encyclopedia of Public International Law*.

United Nations (2000), *Report of the Panel on United Nations Peace Operations*, A/55/305–S/2000/809.

van Genugten, W. (2014), Sleutelen aan "het volkenrechtelijk mandaat", *Nederlands Juristenblad*, vol. 89, no. 37, 2628–2632.

Vlemminx, F. (2019), Commentaar op artikel 90 van de Grondwet, in: E. Hirsch Ballin and G. Leenknegt (eds.), *Artikelsgewijs commentaar op de Grondwet*, https://www.nederlandrechtsstaat.nl/grondwet/artikel.html?artikel=90&categorie=&auteur=&trefwoord=&1=1#.

Weiss, T. (2011), R2P alive and well after Libya, *Ethics and International Affairs*, vol. 25, no. 3, 287–292.

Weller, M. (2018), The Iraq War—2003, in: T. Ruys, O. Corten and A. Hofer (eds.), *The Use of Force in International Law: A Case-based Approach*, Oxford, Oxford University Press, 639–661.

Bibliography

Books and edited volumes

Bellamy, A. and S. McLoughlin (2018), *Rethinking Humanitarian Intervention*, London, Red Globe Press.

Bindenagel, J. (2016), *Internationale Sicherheit im 21 Jahrhundert: Deutschlands internationale Verantwortung*, Bonn, Bundeszentrale für politische Bildung.

Blaise, N. (2017), *R2P et intervention humanitaire: peut-on (ou comment) dépasser la volonté politique du conseil de sécurité?* Limal, Anthemis.

Bradley, C. (ed.) (2019), *The Oxford Handbook of Comparative Foreign Relations Law,* Oxford, Oxford University Press.

Chesterman, S. (2002), *Just War or Just Peace? Humanitarian Intervention and International Law*, Oxford, Oxford University Press.

Coady, C., N. Dobos and S. Sanyal (eds.) (2018), *Challenges for Humanitarian Intervention: Ethical Demand and Political Reality*, Oxford, Oxford University Press.

Corten, O. (2014), *Le droit contre la guerre,* 2nd edition, Paris, Pedone.

Crawford, J. and M. Koskenniemi (eds.) (2015), *The Cambridge Companion to International Law,* Cambridge, Cambridge University Press.

de Wijk, R. (2015), *The Art of Military Coercion*, Amsterdam, Amsterdam University Press/Transaction Books.

Durch, W., J. Larik and R. Ponzio (eds.) (2018), *Just Security in an Undergoverned World,* Oxford, Oxford University Press.

Etzersdorfer, I. and R. Janik (2016), *Staat, Krieg und Schutszverantwortung*, Wien, Ebner & Spiegel.

Ferdinand, P. (2013), *The Position of Russia and China at the UN Security Council in the Light of Recent Crises,* Brussels, European Parliament.

Franck, T. (2002), *Recourse to Force: State Action against Threats and Armed Attacks,* Cambridge, Cambridge University Press.

Gray, C. (2018), *International Law and the Use of Force,* 4th edition, Oxford, Oxford University Press.

Guidero, A. and M. Hallward (2019), *Global Responses to Conflict and Crisis in Syria and Yemen*, Cham, Palgrave Macmillan.

Hehir, A. (2018), *Hollow Norms and the Responsibility to Protect*, Berlin, Springer.

Hinnesbusch, R. and A. Saouli (eds.) (2019), *The War for Syria: Regional and International Dimensions of the Syrian Uprising*, Abingdon, Taylor & Francis.

Hirsch Ballin, E. and G. Leenknegt (eds.) (2019), *Artikelgewijs commentaar op de Grondwet,* www.nederlandrechtsstaat.nl/grondwet.html.

Holt, V., G. Taylor and M. Kelly (2009), *Protecting Civilians in the Context of UN Peacekeeping Operations: Successes, Setbacks and Remaining Challenges,* New York, United Nations.

Kolb, A. (2018), *The UN Security Council Members' Responsibility to Protect*, Berlin, Springer.

Koops, J. *et al.* (eds.) (2015), *The Oxford Handbook of United Nations Peacekeeping Operations,* Oxford, Oxford University Press.

Koskenniemi, M. (2011), *The Politics of International Law,* Oxford, Hart Publishing.

Kreß, C. and S. Barriga (eds.) (2018), *The Crime of Aggression: A Commentary,* Cambridge, Cambridge University Press.

Kuwali, D. and F. Viljoen (eds.) (2016), *Africa and the Responsibility to Protect: Article 4(h) of the African Union Constitution Act*, Abingdon, Routledge.

Larik, J. (2016), *Foreign Policy Objectives in European Constitutional Law,* Oxford, Oxford University Press.

Lawson, M. and E. Morgenstern (2019), *Foreign Aid: An Introduction to U.S. Programs and Policy,* Washington Congressional Research Service.

Nadin, P. (2016), *UN Security Council Reform,* London, Routledge.

Orford, A. and F. Hoffmann (eds.), *The Oxford Handbook for the Theory of International Law,* Oxford, Oxford University Press.

Pattison, J. (2012), *Humanitarian Intervention and the Responsibility to Protect: Who Should Intervene?*, Oxford, Oxford University Press.

Power, S. (2002), *A Problem from Hell: America and the Age of Genocide,* New York, Basic Books.

Rudolf, P. (2017), *Zur legitimität militärischer Gewalt*, Bonn, Bundeszentrale für politische Bildung.

Ruys, T., O. Corten and A. Hofer (eds.) (2018), *The Use of Force in International Law: A Case-Based Approach*, Oxford, Oxford University Press.

Scheid, D. (ed.) (2014), *The Ethics of Armed Humanitarian Intervention*, Cambridge, Cambridge University Press.

Schmitt, M. (ed.) (2017), *Tallinn Manual 2.0 on the International Law Applicable to Cyber Operations,* Cambridge, Cambridge University Press.

Silander, D. and D. Wallace (eds.) (2017), *International Organizations and the Implementation of the Responsibility to Protect: The Humanitarian Crisis in Syria*, Abingdon, Routledge.

Simma, B. *et al.* (eds.) (2012), *The Charter of the United Nations: A Commentary,* vol. 1, 3rd edition, Oxford, Oxford University Press.

Téson, F. (2005), *Humanitarian Intervention: An Inquiry into Law and Morality,* New York, 3rd edition, Transnational Publishers.

Thakur, R. (2006), *The United Nations, Peace and Security: From Collective Security to the Responsibility to Protect,* Cambridge, Cambridge University Press.

Varwick, J. (2017), *NATO in (Un)Ordnung*, Bonn, Bundeszentrale für politische Bildung.

Warren, A. (2018), *Rethinking Humanitarian Intervention in the 21st Century*, Edinburgh, Edinburgh University Press.

Weerdesteijn, M. (2016), *The Rationality of Dictators: Towards a More Effective Implementation of the Responsibility to Protect*, Mortsel, Intersentia.

Weiss, T. (2016), *Humanitarian Intervention: Ideas in Action*, Cambridge, Polity Press.

Weller, M. (2017), *The Oxford Handbook of the Use of Force in International Law*, Oxford, Oxford University Press.

Reports and other official documents

Adviesraad Internationale Vraagstukken en Commissie van advies inzake Volkenrechtelijke vraagstukken /Advisory Council on International Affairs and Advisory Committee on Issues of Public International Law (2000), *Humanitaire interventie/Humanitarian Intervention,* The Hague, AIV Secretariat.

Adviesraad Internationale Vraagstukken /Advisory Council on International Affairs (2004), *Preëmptief optreden/Pre-emptive Action*, The Hague, AIV Secretariat.

Adviesraad Internationale Vraagstukken /Advisory Council on International Affairs (2010), *Nederland en de "Responsibility to Protect": de verantwoordelijkheid om mensen te beschermen tegen massale wreedheden/The Netherlands and the Responsibility to Protect: The Responsibility to Protect People from Mass Atrocities*, The Hague, AIV secretariat.

Adviesraad Internationale Vraagstukken /Advisory Council on International Affairs (2016), *De bescherming van de burgerbevolking in gewapend conflict: over gebaande paden en nieuwe wegen/The Protection of Civilians in Armed Conflict: Well-Trodden Paths and New Ways Forward,* The Hague, AIV secretariat.

Armed Conflict Location & Event Data Project (ACLED) (2019), *ACLED 2018: The Year in Review*, Madison, Wisconsin, ACLED, January 2019.

Ball, N., E. van Veen and M. Price (2015), *Fighting for Peace: The Tricky Business of Using Greater Force in UN Peace Operations,* The Hague, Clingendael Institute.

Commissie van Advies inzake Volkenrechtelijke Vraagstukken /Advisory Committee on Issues of Public International Law and External Advisor on Public International Law (2017), *Joint Advisory Report on the Scope for and the Significance and Desirability of the Use and Term Genocide by Politicians,* The Hague.

Commissie van Advies inzake Volkenrechtelijke Vraagstukken/Advisory Committee on Issues of Public International Law (2018), *The ILC Draft Articles on Crimes Against Humanity*, The Hague.

Commissie van Onderzoek Besluitvorming Irak (2010), *Rapport*, Amsterdam, Boom (summary in English).

Danish Institute for International Studies (2005), *New Threats and the Use of Force*, Gullanders, Bogtrykkeri.

Department for International Development (2017), *Saving Lives, Building Resilience, Reforming the System: the UK Government's Humanitarian Reform Policy*, London.

House of Commons Foreign Affairs Committee (2018), *Global Britain: The Responsibility to Protect*, London, House of Commons Secretariat.

Independent International Commission on Kosovo (2000), *The Kosovo Report: Conflict, International Response, Lessons Learned*, Oxford, Oxford University Press.

Institute for Economics & Peace (2019), *Global Peace Index 2019: Measuring Peace in a Complex World*, Sydney.

International Commission on Intervention and State Sovereignty (2001), *The Responsibility to Protect*, Ottawa, International Development Research Centre.

International Committee of the Red Cross (2012), *Enhancing Protection for Civilians in Armed Conflict and other Situations of Violence*, 2nd edition, Geneva, International Committee of the Red Cross.

International Law Association (2018), *Sydney Conference: Final Report on Aggression and the Use of Force*.

International Law Commission (2018), Report of the International Law Commission, A/73/10, 70th Session, Supp. No. 10, legal.un.org/ilc/reports/2018/english/a_73_10_advance.pdf (Chapter IV on *Subsequent Agreements and Subsequent Practice in Relation to the Interpretation of Treaties*).

Kavanagh, J. *et al.* (2019), *Characteristics of Successful U.S. Military Interventions*, Santa Monica, California, RAND Corporation.

Lewis, D., N. Modirzadeh and G. Blum (The Harvard Law School Program on International Law and Armed Conflict) (2019), *Quantum of Silence: Inaction and Jus ad Bellum*, dash.harvard.edu/bitstream/handle/1/40931878/Quantum%20of%20Silence%202019.pdf?sequence=1&isAllowed=y.

Ministère de l'Europe et des Affaires étrangères/Ministry of Europe and Foreign Affairs (2018), *Stratégie humanitaire de la République française, 2018–2022*, Paris.

Munich Security Conference (2019), *Munich Security Report 2019 The Great Puzzle: Who Will Pick Up the Pieces?*, München, Stiftung Münchner Sicherheitskonferenz.

Netherlands Institute for War Documentation (2002), *Srebrenica, A "Safe" Area – Reconstruction, Background, Consequences and Analyses of the Fall of a Safe Area,* Amsterdam.

Prime Minister's Office, *Syria Action – UK Government Legal Position,* Policy Paper, 14 April 2018.

Report of a Committee of Privy Counsellors (2016), *The Report of the Iraq Inquiry*, London, HMSO ("Chilcot Report").

Schneider, T. and T. Lütkefend (2019), *Nowhere to Hide: the Logic of Chemical Weapons Use in Syria*, Berlin, Global Public Policy Institute.

Sebastián, S. and A. Gorur (2018), *U.N. Peacekeeping and Host-State Consent: How Missions Navigate Relationships with Governments*, Washington D.C., The Stimson Center.

United Nations (2000), *Report of the Panel on United Nations Peace Operations*, A/55/305-S/2000/809.

United Nations (2018), *Responsibility to Protect: From Early Warning to Early Action,* New York, UN Secretariat.

U.S. Mission to the United Nations (1995), *Global Humanitarian Emergencies*, New York, U.S. Mission to the United Nations.

Watts, S., P. Johnston, J. Kavanagh, S. Zeigler, B. Frederick, T. Johnston, K. Mueller, A. Cevallos, N. Chandler, M. Smith, A. Stephenson and J. Thompson (2017), *Limited Intervention: Evaluating the Effectiveness of Limited Stabilization, Limited Strike and Containment Operations,* Santa Monica, RAND.

Articles, contributions to edited volumes and commentaries

Akande, D. and A. Tzanakopoulos (2018), The crime of aggression before the International Criminal Court: introduction to the symposium, *European Journal of International Law*, vol. 29, no. 3, 829–833.

Akpınar, P. (2016), The limits of mediation in the Arab Spring: the case of Syria, *Third World Quarterly*, vol. 37, no. 12, 2288–2303.

Alkopher, T. (2016), From Kosovo to Syria: the transformation of NATO Secretaries General's discourse on military humanitarian intervention, *European Security*, vol. 25, no. 1, 49–71.

Aloyo, E. (2015), Just war theory and the last of last resort, *Ethics & International Affairs*, vol. 29, no. 2, 187–201.

Aloyo, E. (2016), Reconciling just causes for armed humanitarian intervention, *Ethical Theory and Moral Practice*, vol. 19, no. 2, 313–328.

Averre, D. and L. Davies (2015), Russia, humanitarian intervention and the Responsibility to Protect: the case of Syria, *International Affairs*, vol. 91, no. 4, 813–834.

Barber, R. (2018), Uniting for peace not for aggression: responding to chemical weapons in Syria without breaking the law, *Journal of Conflict & Security Law*, vol. 24, no. 1, 71–110.

Bellamy, A. and S. McLoughlin (2019), Human protection and the politics of armed intervention: with responsibility comes accountability, *Global Responsibility to Protect*, vol. 11, no. 3, 333–361.

Benjamin, A. (2018), Syria: the unbearable lightness of intervention, *Wisconsin International Law Journal*, vol. 35, no. 3, 515–548.

Biermann, R. (2014), Legitimitätsprobleme humanitärer Intervention: Kontinuitätslinien zwischen Kosovo und Libyen, *Zeitschrift für Friedens- und Konfliktforschung*, vol. 3, no. 1, 6–42.

Bitensky, S. (2017) For recognition of a people's right to UN authorized intervention to stop mass atrocities, *Washington University Global Studies Law Review*, vol. 16, no. 2, 245–294.

Bleek, P. and N. Kramer (2016), Eliminating Syria's chemical weapons: implications for addressing nuclear, biological, and chemical threats, *The Nonproliferation Review*, vol. 23, no. 1–2, 197–230.

Board of editors (2010), Report of the Dutch Committee of Inquiry on the war in Iraq: chapter 8: the basis in international law for the military intervention in Iraq, *Netherlands International Law Review*, vol. 57, no. 1, 87–137.

Bradley, C. (2019), U.S. war powers and the potential benefits of comparativism, in: C. Bradley (ed.), *The Oxford Handbook of Comparative Foreign Relations Law*, Oxford, Oxford University Press, 753–770.

Brooks, R. (2014), Humanitarian intervention: evolving norms, fragmenting consensus, *Maryland Journal of International Law*, vol. 29, 161–183.

Buchwald, T. (2019), The use of force against "rogue states", *Case Western Reserve Journal of International Law*, vol. 51, no. 1 & 2, 177–188.

Charbonneau, L. and J. Irish. (2015), Dozens of nations back French appeal to limit use of U.N. veto, *Reuters*, 1 October 2015, www.reuters.com/article/us-un-assembly-veto/dozens-of-nations-back-french-appeal-to-limit-use-of-u-n-veto-idUSKCN0RU30V20150930.

Choi, S. (2013), What determines US humanitarian intervention, *Conflict Management and Peace Science*, vol. 30, no. 2, 121–139.

De Beer, A. and D. Tladi (2019), The use of force against Syria in response to alleged use of chemical weapons by Syria: a return to humanitarian intervention?, *Zeitschrift für ausländisches öffentliches Recht und Völkerrecht*, vol. 79, no. 2, 205–240.

Deeks, A. (2012), "Unwilling or Unable": toward a normative framework for extra-territorial self-defense, *Virginia Journal of International Law*, vol. 52, no. 3, 483–550.

Deeks, A. (2018), The NATO intervention in Libya – 2011, in: T. Ruys, O. Corten and A. Hofer (eds.), *The Use of Force in International Law: A Case-Based Approach*, Oxford, Oxford University Press, 749–759.

De Wet, E. (2015), The modern practice of intervention by invitation in Africa and its implications for the prohibition of the use of force, *European Journal of International Law*, vol. 26, no. 4, 979–998.

Dörr, O. (2015), Prohibition of use of force, *Max Planck Encyclopedia of Public International Law*.

Dörr, O. and A. Randelzhofer (2012), Purposes and Principles, Article 2 (4), in: B. Simma *et al.* (eds.), *The Charter of the United Nations: A Commentary*, 3rd edition, Oxford, Oxford University Press, vol. 1, 200–234.

Edwards, B. and M. Cacciatori (2018), The politics of international chemical weapon justice: the case of Syria, 2011–2017, *Contemporary Security Policy*, vol. 39, no. 2, 280–297.

Erameh, N. (2017), Humanitarian intervention, Syria and the politics of human rights protection, *The International Journal of Human Rights*, vol. 21, no. 5, 517–530.

Ercan, P. (2019), UN General Assembly dialogues on the Responsibility to Protect and the use of force for humanitarian purposes, *Global Responsibility to Protect*, vol. 11, no. 3, 313–332.

Everett, A. (2019), Humanitarian military action in the 21st century: three trends shaping the contemporary landscape, *Global Responsibility to Protect*, vol. 11, no. 3, 257–283.

Fabius, L. (2013), Réformer le droit de veto au Conseil de sécurité, *Le Monde*, 4 October 2013, www.lemonde.fr/idees/article/2013/10/04/reformer-le-droit-de-veto-au-conseil-de-securite-par-laurent-fabius_3489782_3232.html.

Field, M. and M. Wright (2018), Russian trolls sent thousands of pro-Leave messages on day of Brexit referendum, Twitter data reveals, *The Telegraph*, 17 October 2018, www.telegraph.co.uk/technology/2018/10/17/russian-iranian-twitter-trolls-sent-10-million-tweets-fake-news/.

Forsythe, D. (2014), The UN Security Council and human rights: promising developments, persistent problems, *Journal of Human Rights*, vol. 13, no. 2, 121–145.

Forteau, M. (2015), Rescuing nationals abroad, in: M. Weller (ed.), *The Oxford Handbook of the Use of Force in International Law*, Oxford, Oxford University Press, 947–961.

Franchini, D. and A. Tzanakopoulus (2018), The Kosovo crisis – 1999, in: T. Ruys, O. Corten and A. Hofer (eds.), *The Use of Force in International Law: A Case-Based Approach*, Oxford, Oxford University Press, 594–622.

Garwood-Gowers, A. (2016), China's responsible protection concept: reinterpreting the Responsibility to Protect (R2P) and military intervention for humanitarian purposes, *Asian Journal of International Law*, vol. 6, no. 1, 89–116.

Gaskarth, J. (2016), The fiasco of the 2013 Syria votes: decline and denial in British foreign policy, *Journal of European Public Policy*, vol. 23, no. 5, 718–734.

Gill, T. (2005), Humanitarian intervention: legality, justice and legitimacy, *Global Community Yearbook of International Law and Jurisprudence*, vol. 1, 51–74.

Ginsburg, T. (2014), Chaining the dog of war: comparative data, *Chicago Journal of International Law*, vol. 15, no. 1, 138–161.

Gramyk, E. (2014), Increased Franco-British military cooperation: the impetus, its results, and the impact on international humanitarian intervention, *San Diego International Law Journal*, vol. 15, no. 2, 377–423.

Hakimi, M. and J. Katz Cogan (2016), The two codes on the use of force, *European Journal of International Law*, vol. 27, no. 2, 257–291.

Halliyadde, M. (2016), Syria: another drawback for R2P: an analysis of R2P's failure to change international law on humanitarian intervention, *Indiana Journal of Law and Social Equality*, vol. 4, no. 2, 215–248.

Hehir, A. and A. Lang, (2015), The impact of the Security Council on the efficiency of the International Criminal Court and the Responsibility to Protect, *Criminal Law Forum*, vol. 26, no. 1, 153–179.

Henderson, C. (2015), The UK government's legal opinion on forcible measures in response to the use of chemical weapons by the Syrian government, *International and Comparative Law Quarterly*, vol. 64, no. 1, 179–196.

Henriksen, A. (2018), Trump's missile strike on Syria and the legality of using force to deter chemical warfare, *Journal of Conflict and Security Law*, vol. 23, no. 1, 33–48.

Henriksen, A. and M. Schack (2014), The crisis in Syria and humanitarian Intervention, *Journal of the Use of Force and International Law*, vol. 1, no. 1, 122–147.

Hersman, R. (2018), Resisting impunity for chemical-weapons attacks, *Survival*, vol. 60, no. 2, 73–90.

Hill, S. and A. Manea (2018), Protection of civilians: a NATO perspective, *Utrecht Journal of International and European Law*, vol. 34, no. 2, 146–160.

Hood, W. (2015), Humanitarian intervention in Syria: is crisis response and limited contingency operations the solution?, *Military Law Review*, vol. 223, no. 3, 610–628.

Howard, L. and A. Stark (2018), How civil wars end: the international system, norms and the role of external actors, *International Security*, vol. 42, no. 3, 127–171.

Junk, J. (2014), The two-level politics of support — US foreign policy and the Responsibility to Protect, *Conflict, Security & Development*, vol. 14, no. 4, 535–564.

Kaarbo, J. and D. Kenealy (2016), No, Prime Minister: explaining the House of Common's vote on intervention in Syria, *European Security*, vol. 25, no. 1, 28–48.

Kaarbo, J. and D. Kenealy (2017), Precedents, parliaments, and foreign policy: historical analogy in the House of Commons vote on Syria, *West European Politics*, vol. 40, no. 1, 62–79.

Karazsia, Z. (2018), An unfulfilled promise: the genocide convention and the obligation of prevention, *Journal of Strategic Security*, vol. 11, no. 4, 20–31.

Kenkel, K. and C. Stefan (2016), Brazil and the 'responsibility while protecting' initiative: norms and the timing of diplomatic support, *Global Governance*, vol. 22, no. 1, 47–78.

Kennedy, D. (2015), Chapter 7: Lawfare and warfare, in: J. Crawford and M. Koskenniemi (eds.), *The Cambridge Companion to International Law*, Cambridge, Cambridge University Press, 158–184.

Kioko, B. (2003), The right of intervention under the African Union's Constitutive Act: from non-interference to non-intervention, *International Review of the Red Cross*, vol. 85, no. 852, 807–825.

Koh, H. (2017), Humanitarian intervention: time for better law, *American Journal of International Law Unbound*, vol. 111, 287–291.

Koskenniemi, M. (2002), "The Lady Doth Protest Too Much": Kosovo and the turn to ethics in international law, *Modern Law Review*, vol. 65, no. 2, 159–175.

Kreß, C. (2017), Wird die humanitäre Intervention strafbar?, *Frankfurter Allgemeine Zeitung*, 9 November 2017.

Kreß, C. (2018), The state conduct element, in: C. Kreß and S. Barriga (eds.) (2018), *The Crime of Aggression: A Commentary*, Cambridge, Cambridge University Press, 412–564.

Kritsiotis, D. (2016), Theorizing international law and force and intervention, in: A. Orford and F. Hoffmann (eds.), *The Oxford Handbook of the Theory of International Law*, Oxford, Oxford University Press, 655–683.

Kunschak, M. (2014), The role of the United Nations Security Council in the implementation of Article 4(h), in: D. Kuwali and F. Viljoen (eds.), *Africa and the Responsibility to Protect: Article 4(h) of the African Union Constitutive Act*, Abingdon, Routledge, 54–68.

Lagerwall, A. (2018), Threats of and actual military strikes against Syria – 2013 and 2017, in: T. Ruys, O. Corten and A. Hofer (2018) (eds.), *The Use of Force in International Law: A Case-Based Approach*, Oxford, Oxford University Press, 828–854.

Le Drian, J. and H. Maas (2019), Who, if not us? An alliance for multilateralism, originally published in the newspaper *Süddeutsche Zeitung*, English version reproduced in: onu.delegfrance.org/Who-if-not-us-An-alliance-for-multilateralism.

Lee, P. and L. Chan (2016), China's and India's perspectives on military intervention: why Africa but not Syria?, *Australian Journal of International Affairs*, vol. 70, no. 2, 179–214.

Lewis, J. and B. Tertrais (2017), The thick red line: implications of the 2013 chemical-weapons crisis for deterrence and transatlantic relations, *Survival*, vol. 59, no. 6, 77–108.

Longo, C. (2016), R2P: an efficient means for intervention in humanitarian crisis: a case study of Isil in Iraq and Syria, *George Washington International Law Review*, vol. 48, no. 4, 893–918.

Lowe, V. and A. Tzanakopoulos (2011), Humanitarian intervention, *Max Planck Encyclopedia of Public International Law.*

Mahapatra, D. (2016), The mandate and the (in)effectiveness of the United Nations Security Council and international peace and security: the contexts of Syria and Mali, *Geopolitics*, vol. 21, no. 1, 43–68.

McCabe, A. (2014), Balancing aggression and compassion in international law: the crime of aggression and humanitarian intervention, *Fordham Law Review*, vol. 83, no. 2, 991–1030.

Melling, G. (2018), Beyond rhetoric: evaluating the Responsibility to Protect as norm of humanitarian intervention, *The Journal of the Use of Force and International Law*, vol. 5, no. 1, 178–196.

Melling, G. and A. Dennett (2018), The Security Council veto and Syria: responding to mass atrocities through the "Uniting for Peace" resolution, *Indian Journal of International Law*, vol. 57, no. 3–4, 285–307.

Mello, P. (2017), Curbing the royal prerogative to use military force: the British House of Commons and the conflicts in Libya and Syria, *West European Politics*, vol. 40, no. 1, 80–100.

Mills, K. (2015), R2P and the ICC: at odds or in sync?, *Criminal Law Forum*, vol. 26, no. 1, 73–99.

Nahlawi, Y. (2016), The Responsibility to Protect and Obama's red line on Syria, *Global Responsibility to Protect*, vol. 8, no. 1, 76–101.

Nahlawi, Y. (2019), Overcoming Russian and Chinese vetoes on Syria through Uniting for Peace, *Journal of Conflict & Security Law*, vol. 24, no. 1, 111–143.

Newman, E. and E. Aloyo (2018), Overcoming the paradox of conflict prevention, in: W. Durch, J. Larik and R. Ponzio (eds.), *Just Security in an Undergoverned World*, Oxford, Oxford University Press, 43–69.

Odeyemi, C. (2016), Re-emerging powers and the impasse in the UNSC over R2P intervention in Syria, *Strategic Analysis*, vol. 40, no. 2, 122–149.

O'Meara, C. (2017), Should international law recognize a right of humanitarian intervention, *International and Comparative Law Quarterly*, vol. 66, no. 2, 441–466.

Orakhelashvili, A. (2015), Changing *jus cogens* through state practice? The case of the prohibition to use force and its exceptions, in: M. Weller (ed.), *The Oxford Handbook of the Use of Force in International Law*, Oxford, Oxford University Press, 157–178.

Pannier, A. (2017), From one exceptionalism to another: France's strategic relations with the United States and the United Kingdom in the post-cold war era, *Journal of Strategic Studies*, vol. 40, no. 4, 475–504.

Paris, R. (2014), The 'Responsibility to Protect' and the structural problems of preventive humanitarian intervention, *International Peacekeeping*, vol. 21, no. 5, 569–603.

Pattison, J. (2017), Perilous noninterventions? The counterfactual assessment of Libya and the need to be a responsible power, *Global Responsibility to Protect*, vol. 9, no. 2, 219–228.

Posner, E. (2011), Outside the law, *Foreign Policy*, 25 October 2011.

Powers, P. (2016), Unilateral humanitarian intervention and reform of the UN veto, *Homeland and National Security Law Review*, vol. 4, no. 1, 79–104.

Qureshi, W. (2018), International law and military intervention: U.S. action in Syria, *University of Hawai'i Law Review*, vol. 40, no. 2, 115–154.

Ralph, J., J. Holland and K. Zhekova, (2017), Before the vote: UK foreign policy discourse on Syria 2011–13, *Review of International studies*, vol. 43, no. 5, 875–897.

Ramsden, M. (2016), Uniting for peace and humanitarian intervention: the authorizing function of the UNGA, *Washington International Law Journal*, vol. 25, no. 2, 267–302.

Raut, B. (2017), An analysis of humanitarian intervention: a case study on the Kosovo crisis, *National Judicial Academy Law Journal*, vol. 11, no. 1, 167–182.

Recchia, S. (2016), Authorising humanitarian intervention: a five-point defence of existing multilateral procedures, *Review of International Studies*, vol. 41, no. 1, 50–72.

Rowe, A. (2018), Soft sovereignty: a possible basis for the legality of humanitarian intervention, *North East Law Review*, vol. 6, 90–111.

Ruys, T. (2018), Criminalizing aggression: how the future of the law on the use of force rests in the hands of the ICC, *European Journal of International Law*, vol. 29, no. 3, 887–917.

Ryngaert, C. and N. Schrijver (2015), Lessons learned from the Srebrenica massacre: from UN peacekeeping reform to legal responsibility, *Netherlands International Law Review*, vol. 62, no. 2, 219–227.

Sarvarian, A. (2016), Humanitarian intervention after Syria, *Legal Studies*, vol. 36, no. 1, 20–47.

Scharf, M. (2019a), Responding to chemical weapons use in Syria, *Case Western Reserve Journal of International Law*, vol. 51, no. 1 & 2, 189–200.

Scharf, M. (2019b), Striking a Grotian moment: how the Syria airstrikes changed international law relating to humanitarian intervention, *Chicago Journal of International Law*, vol. 19, no. 2, 586–614.

Schmitt, M. and C. Ford (2017), Assessing U.S. justifications for using force in response to Syria's chemical attacks: an international law perspective, *Journal of National Security Law and Policy*, vol. 9, no. 2, 283–303.

Stahn, C. (2013), Between law-breaking and law-making: Syria, humanitarian intervention and what the law ought to be, *Journal of Conflict & Security Law*, vol. 19, no. 1, 25–48.

Stavridis, S. (2016), The French parliament and the conflicts in Libya and Syria, *Mediterranean Quarterly*, vol. 27, no. 4, 21–41.

Sterner, E. (2014), Dictators and deterrence: Syria's Assad, chemical weapons, and the threat of U.S. military action, *Comparative Strategy*, vol. 33, no. 5, 407–423.

Sullivan, P. and Koch, M. (2009), Military Intervention by Powerful States 1945–2003, *Journal of Peace Research*, vol. 46, no. 5, 707–718.

Tardy, T. (2015), United Nations Preventive Deployment Force (UNPREDEP – Macedonia), in: J. Koops *et al.* (eds.), *The Oxford Handbook of United Nations Peacekeeping Operations*, Oxford, Oxford University Press, 500–510.

Tertrais, B. (2014), Drawing red lines right, *The Washington Quarterly*, vol. 37, no. 3, 7–24.

Thakur, R. (2016), The Responsibility to Protect at 15, *International Affairs*, vol. 92, no. 2, 415–434.

Tiefer, C. and K. Clark (2016), Congressional and presidential war powers as a dialogue: analysis of the Syrian and ISIS conflicts, *Cornell International Law Journal*, vol. 49, no. 3, 683–722.

Tomuschat, C. (2008), *Uniting for peace, introductory note*, United Nations Audiovisual Library of International Law, legal.un.org/avl/ha/ufp/ufp.html.

Trahan, J. (2015), Defining the 'grey area' where humanitarian intervention may not be fully legal, but is not the crime of aggression, *Journal on the Use of Force and International Law*, vol. 2, no. 1, 42–80.

Trapp, K. (2017), Unauthorized military intervention for the public good: a response to Harold Koh, *American Journal of International Law Unbound*, vol. 111, 292–297.

Trapp, R. (2014), Elimination of the chemical weapons stockpile of Syria, *Journal of Conflict and Security Law*, vol. 19, no. 1, 7–13.

Treves, T. (2006), Customary international law, *Max Planck Encyclopedia of Public International Law*.

Tzeng, P. (2017), Humanitarian intervention at the margins: an examination of recent incidents, *Vanderbilt Journal of Transnational Law*, vol. 50, no. 2, 415–462.

Udoh, A. (2015), Case study: invoking the Uniting for Peace resolution of 1950 to authorize the use of humanitarian military intervention and prevent mass atrocities in Syria, *Willamette Journal of International Law and Dispute Resolution*, vol. 23, no. 1, 187–232.

van Genugten, W. (2014), Sleutelen aan 'het volkenrechtelijk mandaat', *Nederlands Juristenblad*, vol. 89, no. 37, 2628–2632.

Visser, L. (2019), May the force be with you: the legal classification of intervention by invitation, *Netherlands International Law Review*, vol. 66, no. 1, 21–45.

Vlemminx, F. (2019), Commentaar op artikel 90 van de Grondwet, in: E. Hirsch Ballin and G. Leenknegt (eds.), *Artikelgewijs commentaar op de Grondwet*, www.nederlandrechtsstaat.nl/grondwet/artikel.html?artikel=90&categorie=&auteur=&trefwoord=&1=1#.

Weiss, T. (2011), R2P alive and well after Libya, *Ethics and International Affairs*, vol. 25, no. 3, 287–292.

Weller, M. (2018), The Iraq War – 2003, in: T. Ruys, O. Corten and A. Hofer (eds.), *The Use of Force in International Law: A Case-Based Approach*, Oxford, Oxford University Press, 639–661.

Williams P and S. Pearlman (2019), Use of force in human crises, *Case Western Reserve Journal of International Law*, vol. 51, no. 1–2, 211–222.

Blogposts

Byman, D. (2018), Why engage in a proxy war? A state's perspective, 21 May 2018, www.brookings.edu/blog/order-from-chaos/2018/05/21/why-engage-in-proxy-war-a-states-perspective/.

Gurmendi, A., R. Dunkelberg, P. Ingber, P.P. Pilai and E. Pothelet (2018), Mapping states' reactions to the Syria strikes of April 2018, 7 May 2018, www.justsecurity.org/55835/mapping-states-reactions-syria-strikes-april-2018-a-comprehensive-guide/.

Goodman, R. (2017), What do top legal experts say about the Syria strikes?, 7 April 2017, www.justsecurity.org/39712/top-legal-experts-syria-strikes/.

Heller, K. (2018), Why art. 4(h) of the AU's Constitutive Act does not support UHI, 23 April 2018, opiniojuris.org/2018/04/23/why-art-4h-of-the-au-constitutive-act-does-not-support-unilateral-humanitarian-intervention/.

Koh, H. (2013), Syria and the law of humanitarian intervention (part 1: political miscues and U.S. law), 26 September 2016, www.justsecurity.org/1158/koh-syria/.

Koh, H. (2017), Not illegal: but now the hard part begins, 7 April 2017, www.justsecurity.org/39695/illegal-hard-part-begins/.

www.ingramcontent.com/pod-product-compliance
Lightning Source LLC
Chambersburg PA
CBHW031327230926
51848CB00001B/121